handy homework helper

Math

Writer:
Janet Moredock

Consultant:
Joanna O. Masingila, Ph.D.

Publications International, Ltd.

Louis Weber, CEO
Publications International, Ltd.
7373 North Cicero Avenue
Lincolnwood, Illinois 60712

Permission is never granted for commercial purposes.

Manufactured in China.

8 7 6 5 4 3 2 1

ISBN: 0-7853-1955-7

Janet Moredock is a writer and editor with Creative Services Associates, Inc., and specializes in language arts, reading, art history, science, and math. She has served as editor for World Book Encyclopedia and University of Chicago Press and holds a B.A. in English from Wake Forest University.

Joanna O. Masingila, Ph.D., is Assistant Professor of Mathematics and Mathematics Education at Syracuse University. She holds a Doctor of Philosophy in Mathematics Education from Indiana University and has published numerous articles, papers, and text-books on mathematics and mathematics education.

Cover photography: Siede Preis Photography

Models and agencies: McBlaine & Associates, Inc.: Billy Sweeney; **Royal Modeling Management:** Trevor Hocken, Kim Jacobs, Roderick Jordan, Billy Pyroulis, Jessica Shrader.

Illustrations: Peter McMahon

Contents

GREATER VALUES

About This Book

Homework takes time and a lot of hard work. Many students would say it's their least favorite part of the school day. But it's also one of the most important parts of your school career because it does so much to help you learn. Learning gives you knowledge, and knowledge gives you power.

Homework gives you a chance to review the material you've been studying so you understand it better. It lets you work on your own, which can give you confidence and independence. Doing school work at home also gives your parents a way to find out what you're studying in school.

Everyone has trouble with their homework from time to time, and *Handy Homework Helper: Math* can help you when you run into a problem. This book was prepared with the help of educational specialists. It offers quick, simple explanations of the basic material that you're studying in school. If you get stuck on an idea or have trouble finding some information, *Handy Homework Helper: Math* can help clear it up for you. It can also help your parents help you by giving them a fast refresher course in the subject.

This book is clearly organized by the topics you'll be studying in Math. A quick look at the Table of Contents will tell you which chapter covers the area you're working on. You can probably guess which chapter includes what you need and then flip through the chapter until you find it. For even more help finding what you're looking for, look up key words related to what you're studying in the Index. You might find material faster that way, and you might also find useful information in a place you wouldn't have thought to look.

Remember that different teachers and different schools take different approaches to teaching Math. For that reason, we recommend that you talk with your teacher about using this homework guide. You might even let your teacher look through the book so he or she can help you use it in a way that best matches what you're studying at school.

Number Concepts

32
31
30
29
28
27
26
25
24
23
22
21
20
19
18
17
16
15
14
13
12
11
10
9
8
7
6
5
4
3
2
1
0

Place Value

A number represents an amount. We call that amount the **value** of the number. We use written symbols called **numerals** to stand for numbers.

Look at the number line on the left of the page. As you move up the number line, the numbers *increase* (go up) in value. As you move down the number line, the numbers *decrease* (go down) in value. On this number line, the number with the lowest value is zero. The number with the highest value is thirty-two. The numerals printed in red show how our numbering system is based on groups of tens. Notice that **10 ones** make up **ten,** **2 tens** make up **twenty,** and **3 tens** make up **thirty.**

A numeral is made up of one or more **digits.** The numeral 32 has two digits: 3 and 2. The numeral 200 has three digits: 2, 0, and 0. We use the digits 0, 1, 2, 3, 4, 5, 6, 7, 8, and 9 to write all standard numerals. The value of a digit in a numeral depends on its **place.** In the numeral 32, we say that the 3 is in the **tens' place** and the 2 is in the **ones' place.** The 3 has the value of thirty, or 3 tens, and the 2 has the value of two, or 2 ones.

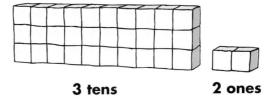

3 tens   **2 ones**

The numeral 365 represents 3 hundreds, 6 tens, and 5 ones. Do you see how the values of the places get smaller as you go from left to right? Hundreds are greater than tens, and tens are greater than ones.

The same digit can have different values, depending on the place it is in.

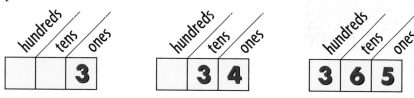

The digit **0** is a placeholder. It is used to show that a certain place in a numeral is empty. For the numeral **10**, you write 0 to show that there are no ones. For the numeral **204**, you write 0 to show that there are no tens.

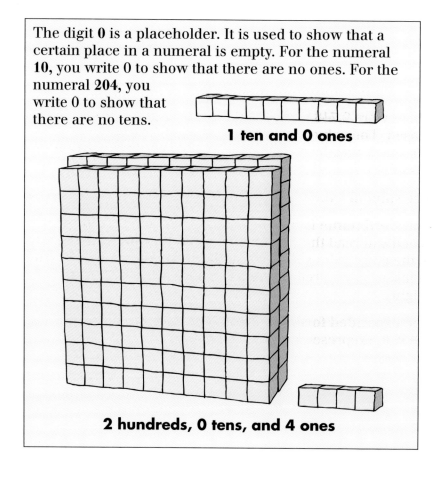

1 ten and 0 ones

2 hundreds, 0 tens, and 4 ones

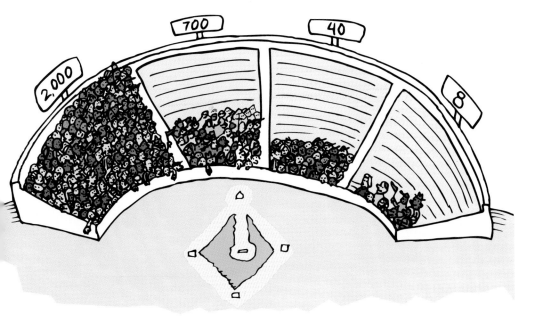

Writing Numbers

There were 2,748 people at the opening game of the baseball season. The value of 2 is **two thousand**. The value of 7 is **seven hundred**. The value of 4 is **forty**. The value of 8 is **eight**. You can write this number in different ways.

The **standard form** of the number is 2,748.

The **word name** is two thousand, seven hundred forty-eight. When you read the word name for 2,748, you say the names of the place values as you read from the left: thousands (two thousand), hundreds (seven hundred), tens (forty), and ones (eight).

The **expanded form** is 2,000 + 700 + 40 + 8. This shows you the value represented by each digit.

Larger Numbers

Most of the places in a numeral are named for numbers that represent groups of ten: tens, hundreds, thousands, and so on. The ones' place is used to represent numbers less than ten. Each place in a numeral is ten times greater in value than the place to its right. For example, it takes 10 ones to make 1 ten; it takes 10 tens to make 1 hundred; and it takes 10 hundreds to make 1 thousand.

What is the word name for the standard form **15,000?** Read the name of the number before the comma (fifteen), and then say the name of the place to the left of the comma (thousand). Fifteen thousand.

What is the word name for **156,351?** Read the name of the number before the comma (one hundred fifty-six), then say the name of the place to the left of the comma (thousand), and then read the number after the comma (three hundred fifty-one). One hundred fifty-six thousand, three hundred fifty-one.

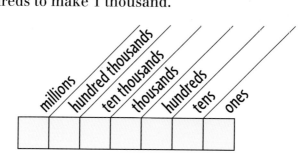

millions	hundred thousands	ten thousands	thousands	hundreds	tens	ones
		1	5	0	0	0
	1	5	6	3	5	1

Different Types of Numbers

Whole numbers are the set of numbers represented by 0, 1, 2, 3, 4, 5, ... (The dots mean that the numbers go on forever in increasing value.)

Counting numbers are the same as the set of whole numbers, except that the counting numbers do not include 0. This makes sense because you always start with 1, not 0, when you count things.

Whole numbers are part of a larger set of numbers called **integers**. Integers are just like whole numbers, except that they include values lower than 0. The numbers to the right of 0 on the number line are called **positive integers**. The numbers to the left of 0 on the number line are called **negative integers**.

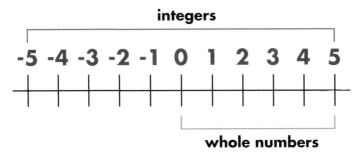

All positive integers have values greater than 0. All negative integers have values less than 0. Negative integers are written just like whole numbers, except that they have a negative sign (-) in front of them. The integer -4 is read "negative four."

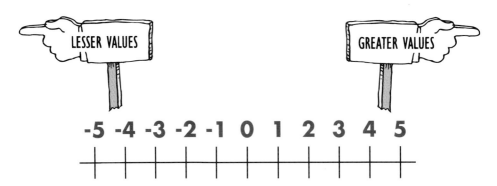

Rational numbers are numbers that can be written in the form of a fraction. A fraction is a number written in the form ᵃ/ᵇ—numbers such as ½, ⅓, and ½. This form tells you that the number above the bar is divided by the number below the bar. (See pages 42–60 for information on fractions.)

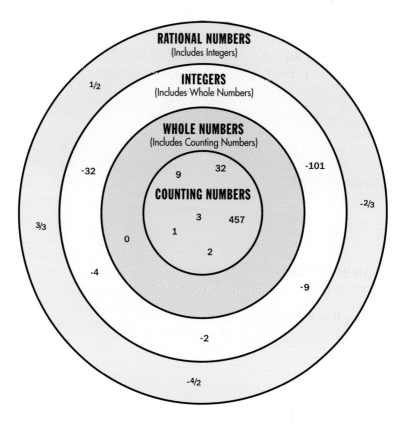

An **even number** is any integer that is divisible by 2. An **odd number** is any integer that is not divisible by 2. Examples of even numbers are 2, 4, 12, and 128. Examples of odd numbers are 3, 5, 13, and 173.

A **prime number** is any integer greater than 1 that is divisible only by itself and 1. A **composite number** is any number that is divisible by a whole number other than itself and 1. For instance, 4 is a composite number because it is divisible by 1, 2, and 4. And 7 is a prime number because it is divisible only by 1 and 7.

Comparing and Ordering Numbers

Some numbers represent larger amounts or greater values than others. For example, you know that 5 represents a greater value than 2. To show that a number has a greater value than another number, we use the "is greater than" symbol (>).

5 > 2 is read "five *is greater than* two."
3 + 3 > 4 is read "three plus three *is greater than* four."

The number sentence 3 + 3 > 4 is true because 3 + 3 = 6, and 6 > 4.

The open end of the "is greater than" symbol always faces the number with the greater value. If we turn the symbol around (<), it is then read "is less than."

5 < 8 is read "five *is less than* eight."
2 + 1 < 7 is read "two plus one *is less than* seven."

When two numbers have the same value, we say they are **equivalent.** We show this by using the "is equal to" or "equals" sign (=).

6 = 6 is read "six *equals* six."
4 + 2 = 6 is read "four plus two *equals* six."

A combination of numerals and other symbols, like 9 - 2 = 7 or 6 > 2, is called a **number sentence** because it states a relationship between numbers.

Is 42 greater than 60? Compare the place values of 42 and 60, starting with the greatest place value, which is tens. 42 has 4 tens. 60 has 6 tens. 6 > 4, so 60 > 42.

If the greatest place values are the same, check the values of the digits in the next, smaller place value to the right. Is 258 greater than 255? Start by comparing the digits at the highest place value, which is hundreds. Both numbers have 2 hundreds. Move to the right and check the next smaller place value, which is tens. Both numbers have 5 tens. Move to the right again and check the ones' place. 258 has 8 ones. 255 has 5 ones. 8 > 5, so 258 > 255.

> For information on comparing and ordering other types of numbers, see the following pages: fractions and mixed numbers, pages 48–50; decimals, pages 64–65; and negative numbers, page 112.

Estimating Numbers

Derrick brought his collection of 248 beetles to his science class for Show and Tell. Derrick's friend Claudio wanted to know how many beetles were in the collection. Derrick answered, "I've collected about 250 beetles." To answer

Claudio's question, Derrick **estimated** the number of beetles in his collection. To estimate is to guess, or to tell "about how much" or "about how many."

A number can have more than one **estimate**, or approximate value. Each of the numbers below is an estimate of 3,173:

3,170   3,200   3,000

When we estimate a number, we compare it to two other numbers: one that has a greater value and one that has a lesser value. We decide which of the two numbers is closer to the exact number, and then we **round up** to the greater number or **round down** to the lesser number. We round down if the exact value is less than halfway between the two numbers. We round up if the exact value is halfway or more between the two numbers.

We get different estimates for a number by rounding to different place values. To round 3,173 to the tens' place, find the values of ten that are nearest to the exact number. There are 7 tens and 3 ones in 3,173, so the number is between 3,170 and 3,180. Because 3,173 is less than halfway between 3,170 and 3,180, we would round it down to 3,170.

To round 3,173 to the hundreds' place, first compare 3,173 to the nearest hundreds values, which are 3,100 and 3,200. Because 3,173 is more than halfway between 3,100 and 3,200, we would round it up to 3,200.

Addition of Whole Numbers

Addition Means...

To **add** means to combine amounts. If there are three apples on a plate and you add two more apples, there will be five apples on the plate.

Addition problems may be written horizontally (across) or vertically (stacked). Both problems below are read "two plus one equals three." We use the plus sign (**+**) to show that we are adding numbers. The equals sign (**=** or **__**) tells us that 2 + 1 and the number 3 have the same value. The numbers we are adding together are called **addends**. The value we get from adding numbers together is called the **sum**.

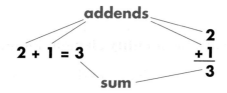

addends

$$2 + 1 = 3 \qquad \begin{array}{r} 2 \\ +1 \\ \hline 3 \end{array}$$

sum

In this section, you will learn about adding whole numbers. For information about adding negative numbers, see pages 112–113.

Properties of Addition

All addition problems share certain **properties**, or features.
The **commutative property of addition** says that changing
the order of the addends does not change the sum.

4 + 3 = 7

3 + 4 = 7

Sometimes, addends are grouped together in parentheses to
make a problem easier to solve. The **associative property of
addition** says that grouping addends differently does not
change the sum.

$$(2 + 2) + 3 = 7 \qquad 2 + (2 + 3) = 7$$

Adding 0 to any number does not change the value of that
number. 0 is called the **identity element for addition**.

$$1 + 0 = 1 \qquad 0 + 298 = 298 \qquad 100 + 0 = 100$$

Adding with a Number Line

You can use a number line to see how addition works for whole numbers. Use the number line below to add six and three. Find the first addend (6) on the number line. To add 3 to 6, count three marks *to the right* of six. The sum of 6 and 3 is 9.

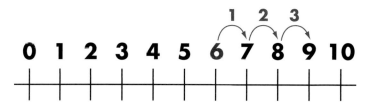

Adding Two-Digit Numbers

To add numbers with two or more digits, you must add the same place values in each addend. In the problem below, add the values in the ones' place of the two addends and write the sum in the ones' column below the equals sign. Then, add the values in the tens' place of the two addends and write the sum in the tens' column below the equals sign.

$$
\begin{array}{r} 14 \\ +11 \\ \hline \end{array}
\qquad
\begin{array}{r} 14 \\ +11 \\ \hline 5 \end{array}
\qquad
\begin{array}{r} 14 \\ +11 \\ \hline 25 \end{array}
$$

Look at the problems below. Do you see anything wrong?

$$
\textbf{A.}\quad \begin{array}{r} 14 \\ +11 \\ \hline \end{array}
\qquad
\textbf{B.}\quad \begin{array}{r} 14 \\ +11 \\ \hline \end{array}
$$

Problem B is written incorrectly because the ones' place in 11 is lined up with the tens' place in 14. In Problem A, the place values are lined up neatly. When you line up your place values carefully, you are less likely to make mistakes in your addition.

Regrouping in Addition

You can write only one digit as the sum for each place value, but sometimes the numbers added together in a column will have a sum that is 10 or greater. When the sum of digits in a certain place value is 10 or greater, you have to **regroup** the sum.

When you add the digits in the ones' column in the problem below, you get 12. You must **regroup** the sum by breaking down 12 into tens and ones. 12 contains 1 ten and 2 ones. Write 2 in the ones' column under the equals sign, and then add the 1 ten to the tens' column by writing 1 at the top of the column. Then, add the digits in the tens' column, including any that you regrouped.

$$
\begin{array}{r} 14 \\ +\ 8 \\ \hline \end{array}
\qquad
\begin{array}{r} {\scriptstyle 1} \\ 14 \\ +\ 8 \\ \hline 2 \end{array}
\qquad
\begin{array}{r} {\scriptstyle 1} \\ 14 \\ +\ 8 \\ \hline 22 \end{array}
$$

**8 + 4 = 12 =
1 ten + 2 ones**

Sometimes regrouping is called **carrying** because we "carry" a digit from one place value to the next larger place value.

Adding Larger Numbers

You may need to regroup more than once while solving an addition problem. For example, you may need to regroup twice when adding three-digit numbers.

First, add the digits in the ones' column and regroup if necessary. Next, add the digits in the tens' column, including any digit you carried from the ones' column. Regroup again if necessary. Finally, add the digits in the hundreds' column. If the last column of digits has a sum of 10 or greater, you do not need to regroup. Simply write the sum on the answer line. The sum of 946 and 157 is 1,103.

$$
\begin{array}{r} 946 \\ +157 \\ \hline \end{array}
\qquad
\begin{array}{r} \overset{1}{9}46 \\ +157 \\ \hline 3 \end{array}
\qquad
\begin{array}{r} \overset{1}{9}\overset{1}{4}6 \\ +157 \\ \hline 03 \end{array}
\qquad
\begin{array}{r} \overset{1}{9}\overset{1}{4}6 \\ +\ 157 \\ \hline 1103 \end{array}
$$

> Notice that the sum in the tens' column is 10. We have 10 tens, which is the same as 100. The tens' place in 100 has a value of zero, so we write 0 in the tens' column of the sum, and carry the 1 hundred to the hundreds' column.

Add numbers with more than three digits the same way. Start by adding the digits in the ones' place and regrouping if necessary. Repeat this step for each of the place values in the addends.

$$
\begin{array}{r} 21,608 \\ +\ 2,905 \\ \hline \end{array}
\qquad
\begin{array}{r} 2\overset{1}{1},608 \\ +\ 2,905 \\ \hline 3 \end{array}
\qquad
\begin{array}{r} 2\overset{1}{1},608 \\ +\ 2,905 \\ \hline 13 \end{array}
$$

$$
\begin{array}{r} \overset{1}{2}1,\overset{1}{6}08 \\ +\ 2,905 \\ \hline 513 \end{array}
\qquad
\begin{array}{r} \overset{1}{2}1,\overset{1}{6}08 \\ +\ 2,905 \\ \hline 4,513 \end{array}
\qquad
\begin{array}{r} \overset{1}{2}1,\overset{1}{6}08 \\ +\ 2,905 \\ \hline 24,513 \end{array}
$$

Sometimes, you will need to add more than two numbers. Write the problem vertically. Make sure that all of the place values are lined up correctly.

$$
\begin{array}{r} \overset{1}{1}3 \\ 37 \\ 5 \\ +\ 4 \\ \hline 59 \end{array}
$$

> Don't forget to add regrouped digits in the column where you have placed them. A common error in addition is forgetting to add digits that have been carried.

Check Your Work

One way to check your addition is to rework the problem with the addends in reverse order. If you get a different answer than you did the first time, check to be sure that you copied the problem correctly. Carefully work the problem again if necessary.

Estimating Sums

You can **estimate** a sum by rounding the addends in a problem. (For more information on rounding numbers, see pages 12–13.)

Malaika is donating part of her mineral and rock collection to the local museum. She wants to give the museum 17 pieces of pyrite, 31 quartz crystals, and 9 geodes. We can estimate the number of items Malaika is donating by rounding each of the addends in the problem below to the nearest ten.

17 + 31 + 9 =

20 + 30 + 10 = 60

The estimated sum, 60, tells you that when you add the exact values of the addends, you will get a sum that is close to 60.

Subtraction of Whole Numbers

Subtraction Means...

To **subtract** means to take the value of one number away from another number. You can use subtraction to **take away** one amount from another amount. If there are eight puppies in a basket and two puppies climb out of the basket, there are six puppies left in the basket.

$$8 - 2 = 6$$

You can also use subtraction to solve **missing addend** problems, to tell you how much more you need. If you want eight puppies in your basket but you only have two, you need six more.

$$8 - 2 = 6$$

You can also use subtraction to **compare** two numbers. If you have one basket with eight puppies and another basket with two puppies, the first basket has six more puppies.

8 – 2 = 6

How to Write Subtraction Problems

You can write subtraction problems horizontally (across) or vertically (stacked). Both problems below are read "five minus two equals three." We use the minus sign (–) to show that we are subtracting the first number from the second number. The equals sign (= or __) tells us that "5 – 2" and "3" have the same value. Each of the numbers in a subtraction problem has a name. The number that is being *subtracted from* is called the **minuend.** The number being *subtracted* is the **subtrahend.** The value we get when we subtract one number from another is called the **difference.**

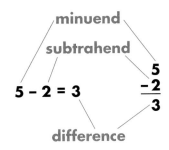

minuend

subtrahend

5 – 2 = 3

$$\begin{array}{r} 5 \\ -2 \\ \hline 3 \end{array}$$

difference

Properties of Subtraction

Addition and subtraction are called **inverse operations** because they are opposites. Subtraction "undoes" addition. If you subtract one addend from the sum in an addition problem, the difference will be the value of the other addend. In the same way, addition is the inverse of subtraction. If you add the difference and the subtrahend in a subtraction problem, the sum will equal the minuend.

$$3 + 4 = 7 \qquad 7 - 4 = 3$$

If you subtract 0 from any number, the difference will be that number. In other words, if you subtract 0 from any minuend, the difference will be the same as the minuend. 0 is the **identity element for subtraction.**

$$19 - 0 = 19 \qquad 2,000 - 0 = 2,000 \qquad 0 - 0 = 0$$

Unlike addition, subtraction does not have a commutative property. If you change the order of the minuend and subtrahend, you change the difference. $5 - 2$ is not the same as $2 - 5$.

Subtraction also does not have an associative property. Grouping numbers differently in a subtraction problem changes the value of the answer.

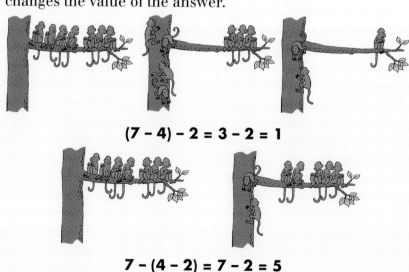

$$(7 - 4) - 2 = 3 - 2 = 1$$

$$7 - (4 - 2) = 7 - 2 = 5$$

Subtracting with a Number Line

You can use a number line to see how subtraction works for whole numbers. Use the number line below to subtract 4 from 7. Find the minuend (7) on the number line. To subtract 4 from 7, count four marks *to the left* of seven. The difference of 7 and 4 is 3.

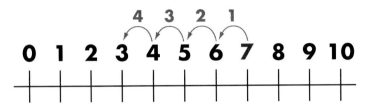

Subtracting Two-Digit Numbers

To subtract numbers with two or more digits, you must subtract the same place values in the minuend and subtrahend.

In the problem below, subtract the value in the ones' place of the subtrahend from the value in the ones' place of the minuend, and write the difference in the ones' column below the equals sign. Then, do the same for the tens' place.

```
 25      25      25
-12     -12     -12
                  3      13
```

> Look at the problems below. Do you see anything wrong?
>
> **A.**   25   **B.**   25
>   -12   -12
>
> Problem A is written incorrectly because the ones' place in 12 is lined up with the tens' place in 25. In Problem B, the place values are lined up neatly. When you line up your place values carefully, you are less likely to make mistakes in your subtraction.

Sometimes, you will get a difference of 0 in the last column on the left. You do not need to write this 0 in your answer.

```
 16
-11
  5
```

If a 0 appears in any column **before** the last column on the left, you must write the 0 in your answer.

```
 23
-13
 10
```

If a place value in the subtrahend has no digit, then that place has a value of 0. Just bring down the digit in the minuend, and write it below the equals sign.

```
  48
-  5
  43
```

Regrouping in Subtraction

If a digit in the minuend you are subtracting from is too small, you need to **regroup** the minuend. In the problem below, you cannot subtract the ones' value in the subtrahend from the ones' value in the minuend. Regroup 23 by borrowing 1 ten from the tens' place and adding it to the 3 ones. You now have 13 ones in the ones' place. Now you can subtract the ones' value of the subtrahend.

```
   23        ¹            ¹
            2̶¹3          2̶¹3
 -  6      -  6        -  6
                         1 7
```

In some problems, you need to subtract from a 0 in the minuend. In the problem below, you have to regroup the minuend by borrowing a ten from the tens' place and adding it to the ones' place. After you regroup in the problem below, the minuend will have 3 tens in the tens' place and 10 ones in the ones' place.

```
            3            3
   40      4̶¹0          4̶¹0
 -18      -1 8        -1 8
                        2 2
```

Borrowing Across Zeros

Sometimes you must take a value from one place value and move it over several other place values to get it where you need it. The problem below shows how to **borrow across zeros** when subtracting. You cannot subtract 5 from 1, so you need to add a ten to the ones' place. There are 0 tens in the minuend, however, and there are 0 hundreds, so you must borrow a ten from the thousands' place. To do this, you must move one place value at a time, starting with the thousands. Take 1 thousand from the thousands' place and add it to the hundreds' place, leaving 1 thousand and 10 hundreds. Then, move 1 hundred to the tens' place, leaving 9 hundreds and 10 tens. Finally, move 1 ten from the tens' place, leaving 9 tens and 11 ones. Then, subtract the subtrahend from the minuend.

$$
\begin{array}{r}
2{,}001 \\
-\ 185 \\
\end{array}
\qquad
\begin{array}{r}
{}^{1} \\
\cancel{2}{,}{}^{1}001 \\
-\ 185 \\
\end{array}
\qquad
\begin{array}{r}
{}^{1}\ \ {}^{9} \\
\cancel{2}{,}{}^{1}\cancel{0}{}^{1}01 \\
-\ 185 \\
\end{array}
$$

$$
\begin{array}{r}
{}^{1}\ {}^{9}\ {}^{9} \\
\cancel{2}{,}{}^{1}\cancel{0}{}^{1}\cancel{0}{}^{1}1 \\
-\ 185 \\
\end{array}
\qquad
\begin{array}{r}
{}^{1}\ {}^{9}\ {}^{9} \\
\cancel{2}{,}{}^{1}\cancel{0}{}^{1}\cancel{0}{}^{1}1 \\
-\ 185 \\
\hline
1{,}816 \\
\end{array}
$$

> There is a shortcut that can make borrowing across zeros easier. You can add a borrowed ten to the digit in the ones' place by simply subtracting 1 from the number formed by the digits to the left of the ones' place.
>
> $$
> \begin{array}{r}
> {}^{1}\ {}^{9}{}^{9} \\
> 2{,}\cancel{00}{}^{1}1 \\
> -\ 185 \\
> \hline
> 1{,}816 \\
> \end{array}
> $$

Check Your Work

You can check your answer in a subtraction problem by adding the difference to the subtrahend. The sum of these two numbers should be the same as the minuend. If the sum does not equal the minuend, check to be sure you have written the subtraction problem correctly, and then work it again carefully.

Estimating Differences

You can **estimate** a difference by rounding the minuend and the subtrahend in a problem. (For more information on rounding numbers, see pages 12–13.)

Nathan's and Grace's pottery class made 138 flower pots and vases to sell at the arts and crafts fair. On the first day of the fair, they sold 96 of the pots and vases. About how many were left?

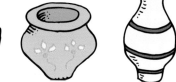

138 – 96 =

140 – 100 = 40

The estimated difference tells you that when you subtract the exact values of the minuend and subtrahend, you will arrive at a difference that is close to 40.

Multiplication of Whole Numbers

Multiplication Means ...

Multiplication is a quick way to add equal numbers. When you multiply, you are really adding the same number repeatedly. For example, if you add 2 to itself 3 times, it is the same as multiplying 2 by 3.

We can use an **array** to see how multiplication works. An array shows things arranged in equal rows and columns. To find the total number of caps in the array on the right, multiply the number of caps in each column (4) by the number of columns (3).

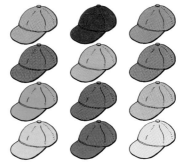

Sometimes you may want to combine items in one set with items in a second set. You can multiply to find out how many

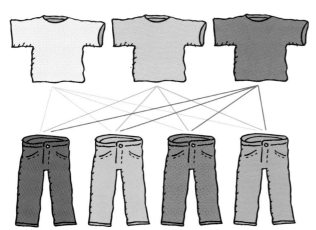

combinations of items are possible. If you had 3 T-shirts and 4 pairs of pants, you would find the total number of outfits you could wear by multiplying the number of T-shirts (3) by the number of pairs of pants (4).

How to Write Multiplication Problems

Multiplication problems can be written horizontally (across) or vertically (stacked). Both problems below are read "three times six equals eighteen." We use the multiplication sign, or times sign, (**x**) to show that we are multiplying numbers. The numbers that are multiplied are called **factors.** The value we get from multiplying two numbers is called the **product.**

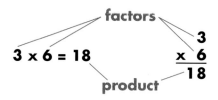

$$3 \times 6 = 18 \qquad \begin{array}{r} 3 \\ \times\ 6 \\ \hline 18 \end{array}$$

Properties of Multiplication

All multiplication problems share certain properties, or features. The **commutative property of multiplication** says that changing the order of the factors does not change the product.

$$2 \times 6 = 12 \qquad 6 \times 2 = 12$$

The **associative property of multiplication** says that grouping factors in different ways does not change the product.

(3 x 4) x 2 = 12 x 2 = 24

3 x (4 x 2) = 3 x 8 = 24

The **distributive property of multiplication over addition** says that if one factor is a sum, multiplying each addend before adding does not change the value of the product.

$$4 \times (10 + 5) = 4 \times 15 = 60$$
$$(4 \times 10) + (4 \times 5) = 40 + 20 = 60$$

The product of any number and 1 is that number. 1 is the **identity element for multiplication.**

$$8 \times 1 = 8 \qquad 1 \times 45 = 45 \qquad 1 \times 1 = 1$$

The product of any number and 0 is 0.

$$99 \times 0 = 0 \qquad 0 \times 32 = 0 \qquad 0 \times 0 = 0$$

Multiplying a Two-Digit Factor by a One-Digit Factor

To multiply a two-digit factor by a one-digit factor, multiply each digit in the top factor by each digit in the bottom factor. Start by multiplying the digits in the ones' column first. Write the product under the equals sign in the ones' column. Then, multiply the tens' digit in the top factor by the bottom factor, and write the answer under the equals sign in the tens' column.

$$
\begin{array}{r} 14 \\ \times\ 2 \\ \hline \end{array}
\qquad
\begin{array}{r} 14 \\ \times\ 2 \\ \hline 8 \end{array}
\qquad
\begin{array}{r} 14 \\ \times\ 2 \\ \hline 28 \end{array}
$$

Regrouping in Multiplication

You can write only one digit as the product for each place value, but sometimes the factors in a column will have a product that is 10 or greater. When the product of digits in a certain place value is 10 or greater, you have to **regroup** the product.

When you multiply the digits in the ones' column in the problem on the next page, you get 20. You must regroup the product by breaking 20 into 2 tens and 0 ones. Write the ones' digit under the equals sign in the ones' column, and carry the tens' digit to the top of the tens' column. Next, multiply the tens' digit in the top factor by the bottom factor. Then, *add* the 2 tens that were carried. The product of 4 and 25 is 100.

```
                    2                2
    25             25               25
  x  4           x  4             x    4
                    0              100
```

$4 \times 5 = 20$ $4 \times 2 = 8;$
$8 + 2 = 10$

Multiplying Two-Digit Factors

To multiply two-digit factors, multiply each digit in the top factor by each digit in the bottom factor. Start by multiplying each digit in the top factor by the ones' digit in the bottom factor and writing the products below the equals sign. Next, multiply each digit in the top factor by the tens' digit in the bottom factor, and write the products below the first line of your answer. Write the first product in the tens' column since you are multiplying by the tens' digit. Make sure the place values are lined up correctly. Then, add the two products together to find the total product. The product of 24 and 13 is 312.

```
     1                1
    24               24               24
   x13              x13              x13
     2               72               72
                                       4
```

$3 \times 4 = 12$ $3 \times 2 + 1 = 7$ $1 \times 4 = 4$

```
    24               24
  x  13            x  13
     72               72
  + 24             + 24
                     312
```

$1 \times 2 = 2$ $72 + 240 = 312$

The number of digits in the bottom factor tells how many rows of products you will need to add in order to find the total product.

Multiplying Three-Digit Factors

To multiply three-digit factors, follow the same steps used in solving two-digit multiplication problems. The first step is to multiply all digits in the top factor by the ones' digit in the bottom factor. The second step is to multiply all digits in the top factor by the tens' digit in the bottom factor. The third step is to multiply all digits in the top factor by the hundreds' digit in the bottom factor. The final step is to add the three products to find the total product.

```
    507            507            507              507
  x 138          x 138          x 138          x   138
   4056           4056           4056             4056
                  1521           1521             1521
                                  507            +507
                                                69,966
```

When multiplying by 10, simply place a 0 after the other factor to find the product.

8 x 10 = 80   15 x 10 = 150   20 x 10 = 200

When multiplying by 100, add two 0s after the other factor.

4 x 100 = 400   21 x 100 = 2,100
10 x 100 = 1,000

When multiplying by 1,000, add three 0s after the other factor.

8 x 1,000 = 8,000   100 x 1,000 = 100,000
1 x 1,000 = 1,000

Whenever you multiply by 2, the product will always be even.

2 x 3 = 6   2 x 9 = 18   2 x 50 = 100

Whenever you multiply by 5, the product will always have a 0 or 5 as the digit in ones' place.

5 x 6 = 30   5 x 9 = 45   5 x 110 = 550

Check Your Work

One way to check multiplication problems is to change the order of the factors and rework the problem. The product should not change. If you get a different product, rework the problem and check it again.

```
      21                48
  x   48            x   21
     168                48
  +  84            +   96
   1,008             1,008
```

Another way to check your work in multiplication is to use division. You can learn more about division on pages 33–41.

Estimating Products

You can **estimate** a product by rounding one of the factors in the problem. (For more information on rounding numbers, see pages 12–13.)

Cara helps her aunt and uncle by picking fruit in their orchard during the summer. One day she picked 4 bushels of apples. One bushel held 127 apples. We can estimate the number of apples Cara picked by rounding one of the factors to the nearest ten. This tells us that Cara picked about 520 apples.

```
    1
   130
  x  4
   520
```

Division of Whole Numbers

Division Means...

Division is a way of separating something into parts or groups of the same size. Division can be thought of as repeated subtraction or as sharing.

Lisa has 12 water balloons, and she's going to throw four balloons at each of her brothers. To find out how many brothers she has, you would divide the number of water balloons (12) by the number of balloons she throws at each brother (4). You can do this by subtracting 4 from 12 as many times as you can. You can subtract 4 from 12 three times, so you know she has 3 brothers.

$$
\begin{array}{r} 12 \\ -\ 4 \\ \hline 8 \end{array}
\qquad
\begin{array}{r} 8 \\ -\ 4 \\ \hline 4 \end{array}
\qquad
\begin{array}{r} 4 \\ -\ 4 \\ \hline 0 \end{array}
$$

Lisa decided she wanted to share her water balloons with her 3 brothers instead of throwing them. To find out how many balloons each of them would get, you would divide the number of balloons (12) by the number of people (4). You can do this by putting the 12 balloons into 4 equal groups. Each of the groups has 3 water balloons in it, so each person would get 3 water balloons.

How to Write Division Problems

We can write division problems horizontally (across) or in long division. Both problems below are read "6 divided by 3 equals 2." In a horizontal problem, the division sign (÷) shows we are dividing the number on the left by the number on the right. In long division, the division sign ($\overline{)}$) shows we are dividing the number on the inside by the number on the outside. Each of the numbers in a division problem has a name. The number that is being divided is called the **dividend.** The number that the dividend is divided by is called the **divisor.** The value we get when we divide one number by another is called the **quotient.**

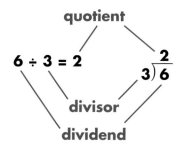

Properties of Division

Division and multiplication are called **inverse operations** because they are opposites. Division "undoes" multiplication. If you multiply the quotient in a division problem by the divisor, the product will be the value of the dividend. If you divide the product of a multiplication problem by one of the factors, the quotient will be the value of the other factor.

$$12 \div 3 = 4 \qquad 4 \times 3 = 12$$

The quotient of any number (except 0) divided by 1 is that number. 1 is the **identity element for division.**

$$8 \div 1 = 8 \qquad 1,000 \div 1 = 1,000 \qquad 1 \div 1 = 1$$

The quotient of any number (except 0) divided by itself is 1.

$$96 \div 96 = 1 \qquad 1 \div 1 = 1 \qquad 1,000,000 \div 1,000,000 = 1$$

The quotient of 0 divided by any nonzero number is 0. This is true because the product of any number and 0 is 0.

$$0 \div 1 = 0 \qquad 0 \div 16 = 0 \qquad 0 \div 1,000,000 = 0$$

Division by 0 is said to be **undefined** because no number can be divided by 0. If you try to solve the problem $6 \div 0$, you will see that you cannot do it. No matter how many times you combine 0, you will never get a product of 6. This is true because the product of 0 and any number is *always* 0. To show that the solution to an equation is an "empty set," a set that contains *no* solution, use the symbol ϕ.

$$42 \div 0 = \phi \qquad 1 \div 0 = \phi \qquad 365 \div 0 = \phi$$

Long Division

We can use place value blocks to show how division works with larger numbers. To divide 66 by 3, divide 66 into 3 equal groups. The blocks below represent 66: 6 tens and 6 ones.

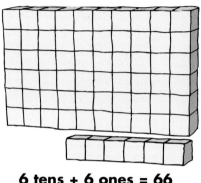

6 tens + 6 ones = 66

First, divide the tens' blocks into three equal groups. These groups will have 2 tens' blocks each, or 20.

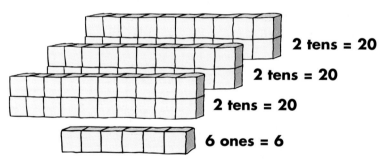

2 tens = 20

2 tens = 20

2 tens = 20

6 ones = 6

Then share the 6 ones equally among the groups of tens' blocks. Each group will have 2 tens plus 2 ones, or 22.

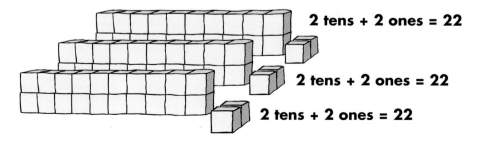

2 tens + 2 ones = 22

2 tens + 2 ones = 22

2 tens + 2 ones = 22

This time, we will solve a problem using long division while also finding the answer with the place value blocks. To divide

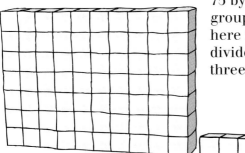

75 by 3, divide 75 into 3 equal groups. The blocks shown here represent 75. First, divide the tens' blocks into three equal groups.

$$3\overline{)75}$$

These groups will have 2 tens' blocks each, or 20, and there will be 1 left over. In the problem, write 2 in the quotient above the tens' place in the dividend to represent the 2 tens in each of the three groups of blocks. Remember that division is really "repeated subtraction." The 6 tens' blocks represent the amount you have "taken away" from 75. In the problem, you also need to subtract 6 tens from the dividend. Do this by multiplying 2 and 3, and subtracting the product from the tens' place in the dividend. The difference that you get (1) represents the 1 ten left over in the place value blocks.

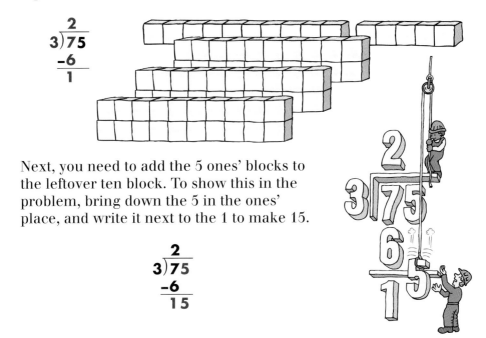

$$
\begin{array}{r}
2 \\
3\overline{)75} \\
-6 \\
\hline
1
\end{array}
$$

Next, you need to add the 5 ones' blocks to the leftover ten block. To show this in the problem, bring down the 5 in the ones' place, and write it next to the 1 to make 15.

$$
\begin{array}{r}
2 \\
3\overline{)75} \\
-6 \\
\hline
15
\end{array}
$$

Share the 15 ones' blocks equally among the three groups. This is the same as dividing 15 by 3. You will add 5 ones' blocks to each of the three groups. To show this in the problem, write 5 in the quotient above the ones' place in the dividend. To find out what is left over, multiply 5 and 3, and subtract the product from 15. The difference is 0, and we have 0 blocks left, so we know we have completed the division.

$$
\begin{array}{r}
25 \\
3\overline{)75} \\
-6 \\
\hline
15 \\
-15 \\
\hline
0
\end{array}
$$

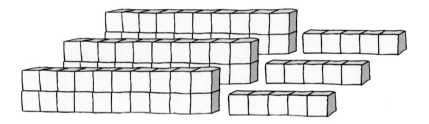

Remainders

Sometimes the divisor will not divide **evenly** into the dividend. This means that there is a **remainder,** or an amount **left over** after the division has been carried out. Start the problem **4)63** by dividing the divisor (4) into the digit in the largest place value of the dividend (6). Divide 4 into 6, and you get a value of 1 with 2 left over. Next, bring down the digit 3 from the dividend, and you get a value of 23 left to be divided. Then, divide 4 into 23, and you get a value of 5 with 3 left over. There are no more digits to bring down from the dividend. Check to be sure the remainder is less than the divisor, and then write the remainder beside the quotient. The "R" stands for "remainder."

$$\begin{array}{r} 1 \\ 4\overline{)63} \\ -4 \\ \hline 2 \end{array} \qquad \begin{array}{r} 15 \text{ R3} \\ 4\overline{)63} \\ -4 \\ \hline 23 \\ -20 \\ \hline 3 \end{array}$$

Why should the remainder be smaller than the divisor? When the remainder is smaller than the divisor and there are no more digits to bring down from the dividend, you know that you have carried the division as far as you can. If you have a remainder that is larger than the divisor, it means that the quotient is too small.

Dividing Dividends with Three or More Digits

Follow the same steps for dividing dividends with three or more digits that you used for dividing two-digit dividends. In the problem below, 6 will not divide into the first digit of the dividend, 1, so you have to divide 6 into the first **two** digits of the dividend, 12. Divide 6 into 12, and you get a value of 2 with 0 left over. Write the quotient above the *second* digit in the dividend (2) to show that you divided 6 into the first two digits. Next, bring down the next digit to the right in the dividend, which is 1, and you get a value of 1 to be divided. Again, 6 will not divide into 1, so you get a value of 0 with 1 left over. Bring down the next digit in the dividend, which is 6, and you get a value of 16 to be divided. Divide 6 into 16 to get a value of 2 with 4 left over. There are no more digits to bring down, and the remainder is less than the quotient. The division is done, and you can write the remainder next to the quotient.

$$6\overline{)1,216} \qquad \begin{array}{r} 2 \\ 6\overline{)1,216} \\ -12 \\ \hline 0 \end{array} \qquad \begin{array}{r} 20 \\ 6\overline{)1,216} \\ -12 \\ \hline 01 \\ 0 \\ \hline 1 \end{array} \qquad \begin{array}{r} 202\text{R4} \\ 6\overline{)1,216} \\ -12 \\ \hline 01 \\ -\ 0 \\ \hline 16 \\ -12 \\ \hline 4 \end{array}$$

Dividing with Two-Digit Divisors

Dividing with two-digit divisors is like dividing with single-digit divisors. 13 will not divide into the first digit (2), but it will divide into the first two digits (27). Remember to write the quotient above the second digit to show that you started by dividing into the first two digits. Complete the division.

$$
13\overline{)275}
\qquad
\begin{array}{r}
2 \\
13\overline{)275} \\
-26 \\
\hline
1
\end{array}
\qquad
\begin{array}{r}
21\ \text{R2} \\
13\overline{)275} \\
-26 \\
\hline
15 \\
-13 \\
\hline
2
\end{array}
$$

With two-digit divisors, you may need to begin by dividing into the first three digits of the divisor. In this problem, 96 will not divide into 1 or 12, but it will divide into 127.

$$
\begin{array}{r}
13\ \text{R30} \\
96\overline{)1{,}278} \\
-\ 96 \\
\hline
318 \\
-\ 288 \\
\hline
30
\end{array}
$$

Check Your Work

You can use multiplication to check your work in division. Simply multiply the quotient by the divisor. The product should be the same as the dividend.

$$
\begin{array}{r}
234 \\
4\overline{)936} \\
-8 \\
\hline
13 \\
-12 \\
\hline
16 \\
-16 \\
\hline
0
\end{array}
\qquad
\begin{array}{r}
11 \\
234 \\
\times\quad 4 \\
\hline
936
\end{array}
$$

Estimating Quotients

Sometimes it is helpful to **estimate** a quotient. You can do this by rounding the dividend or divisor so that they are **compatible numbers**, or numbers that can be easily divided. (For more information about rounding numbers, see pages 12–13.)

Tom Sawyer got 8 friends to whitewash the fence for him. If the whole fence is 118 feet long, about how much of the fence will each friend have to paint?

Find a number close to 118 that 8 will divide into easily. If you round 118 up to 120, you can estimate that each friend will paint less than 15 feet of the fence.

$$118 \div 8 =$$

$$120 \div 8 = 15$$

You can use compatible numbers to find a range of quotients. To find a range for the problem above, find a number less than 118 that 8 will divide into easily. If you round 118 down to 96, you can estimate that each friend will paint more than 12 feet of fence.

$$96 \div 8 = 12$$

Fractions

A Fraction Is...

A fraction is a way of expressing a relationship between two numbers. Fractions can represent several kinds of relationships.

Often, we use fractions to represent a portion of something. In fact, fractions can represent portions of anything that can be divided into equal groups. A fraction can represent part of a group, such as 4 out of

6 of the fish in an aquarium. A fraction can also represent part of a known distance. For example, the distance between 0 and 4 on a number line is part of the distance between 0 and 10.

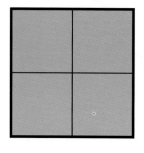

Fractions can also represent parts of objects, figures, or amounts that have been divided into equal parts. This square, for example, has been divided into equal parts. One square has been divided into four equal parts, or 1 ÷ 4.

How to Write Fractions

Most fractions are written in the forms shown below. A fraction has two parts, called **terms.** The top, or first, part is called the **numerator.** The bottom, or second, part is called the **denominator.** The denominator tells how many equal parts something has been divided into. The numerator tells how many of those parts are being considered.

⅔ **of the balls are round**

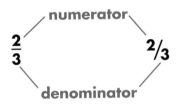

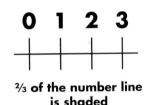

⅔ **of the number line is shaded**

In a **proper fraction,** the numerator is smaller than the denominator. In an **improper fraction,** the numerator is larger than the denominator. Proper fractions represent less than a whole. Improper fractions represent one or several wholes plus part of another.

Improper fraction
¹²⁄₈ **of a pizza had mushrooms**

Proper fraction
⁴⁄₈ **of a pizza had no mushrooms**

Jeanne ordered two pizzas to share with her friends. One of her friends does not like mushrooms, but the others do. Jeanne ordered one pizza with mushrooms and one pizza that had mushrooms on only four slices. Each pizza contained eight slices. What fraction of the pizza contained mushrooms? What fraction didn't have mushrooms?

Equivalent Fractions

Fractions with different denominators may represent the same amount. Fractions that represent the same amount are called **equivalent fractions**. Each figure below is the same size, but each is divided into equal parts of different sizes— halves, fourths, and eighths. The fractions ½, ²⁄₄, and ⁴⁄₈ are equivalent fractions.

$$\frac{1}{2}$$

$$\frac{2}{4}$$

$$\frac{4}{8}$$

To find equivalent fractions, multiply the numerator and denominator of a fraction by the same number. The number sentences below show that ⅓, ²⁄₆, ³⁄₉, ⁴⁄₁₂, and ⁵⁄₁₅ are equivalent fractions.

$$\frac{1 \times 2}{3 \times 2} = \frac{2}{6} \qquad \frac{1 \times 3}{3 \times 3} = \frac{3}{9}$$

$$\frac{1 \times 4}{3 \times 4} = \frac{4}{12} \qquad \frac{1 \times 5}{3 \times 5} = \frac{5}{15}$$

A fraction that has the same number in the numerator and denominator (¹⁄₁, ²⁄₂, ³⁄₃, and so on) has a value of 1. Remember that fractions are another way of showing division, so ³⁄₃ = 3 ÷ 3 = 1. That's why multiplying the numerator and denominator of a fraction by the same number gives you an equivalent fraction.

Simplifying Fractions

Factors are the numbers that can be multiplied to give a certain product, or answer. The factors of 8 are the whole numbers that can be multiplied to give 8 as their product.

$$1 \times 8 = 8 \qquad 2 \times 4 = 8$$

The factors of 8 are 1, 2, 4, and 8.

$$1 \times 6 = 6 \qquad 2 \times 3 = 6$$

The factors of 6 are 1, 2, 3, and 6.

Numbers may share one or more factors. We call factors that are shared **common factors.** The list above shows that 6 and 8 have two common factors—1 and 2. The **greatest common factor,** or **GCF,** is the shared factor with the greatest value. The GCF of 6 and 8 is 2.

What is the GCF of 16 and 20? The common factors of 16 and 20 are 1, 2, and 4. The GCF of 16 and 20 is 4.

$$1 \times 16 = 16 \qquad 1 \times 20 = 20$$

$$2 \times 8 = 16 \qquad 2 \times 10 = 20$$

$$4 \times 4 = 16 \qquad 4 \times 5 = 20$$

You may be able to **simplify** a fraction by dividing its terms (the numerator and denominator) by a common factor. This makes the numbers in the numerator and denominator smaller and easier to work with. Dividing by the GCF puts the fraction in its **simplest terms.** A fraction is in simplest terms when 1 is the only common factor of the numerator and denominator.

There are 24 members in the Astronomy Club. 6 of the members have their own telescopes. What fraction of the members have their own telescopes? ⁶⁄₂₄ of the members have their own telescopes. To simplify the answer to this problem, find the GCF of the numerator (6) and denominator (24), and then divide by it.

$$\frac{6 \div 6}{24 \div 6} = \frac{1}{4}$$

1 is the only shared factor of the numerator and denominator in the new fraction, which means that it is in simplest terms. ¼ of the members of the Astronomy Club have their own telescopes.

Mixed Numbers

A **mixed number** is a number that combines an integer and a fraction. A mixed number represents one or more wholes plus part of another. You can change mixed numbers into improper fractions, and you can change improper fractions into mixed numbers.

To change $4\frac{1}{2}$ to an improper fraction, first multiply the integer (4) and the denominator of the fraction (2). Next, add the product (8) to the numerator of the fraction (1). Then, write the sum (9) over the denominator (2).

$$4 \times 2 = 8$$

$$8 + 1 = 9$$

$$4\frac{1}{2} = \frac{9}{2}$$

Remember this formula to help you convert mixed numbers to improper fractions:

$$\frac{(\text{Integer} \times \text{Denominator}) + \text{Numerator}}{\text{Denominator}} = \frac{\text{Improper}}{\text{Fraction}}$$

To change an improper fraction to a mixed number, first divide the numerator by the denominator. The quotient will be the integer in the mixed number. If there is a remainder, write it above the denominator to form the fraction in the mixed number. For example, if you are changing $\frac{16}{3}$ to a mixed number, divide 3 into 16 to find the integer (5). Write the remainder (1) over the denominator (3) to form the fraction. The mixed number is $5\frac{1}{3}$.

Comparing and Ordering Fractions

It is easy to put fractions in order of value when they have the same denominator. To put the fractions below in order, you simply compare the values of the numerators.

$$\frac{99}{100} \qquad \frac{225}{100} \qquad \frac{1}{100}$$

1 < 99 and 1 < 225 and 99 < 225

$$\frac{1}{100} < \frac{99}{100} < \frac{225}{100}$$

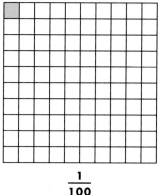

$$\frac{1}{100}$$

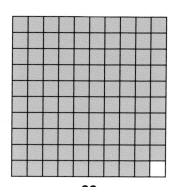

$$\frac{99}{100}$$

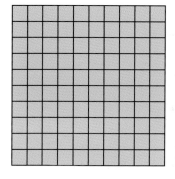
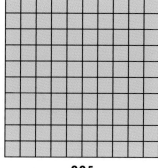
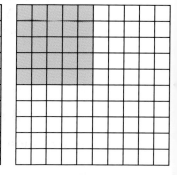

$$\frac{225}{100}$$

To compare the values of fractions that have *unlike* (different) denominators, you may need to change them to fractions that have the same denominator. To do this, you need to know how to find **multiples.** A multiple is the product of a certain number and another number. The list below shows some of the multiples of 2 — 2, 4, 6, 8, 10, 12.

$$2 \times 1 = 2 \qquad 2 \times 4 = 8$$

$$2 \times 2 = 4 \qquad 2 \times 5 = 10$$

$$2 \times 3 = 6 \qquad 2 \times 6 = 12$$

Common multiples are multiples that are shared by two or more numbers. Compare the multiples of 3 shown below to the multiples of 2. You'll see that the common multiples of 3 and 2 that are shown here are 6 and 12.

$$3 \times 1 = 3 \qquad 3 \times 4 = 12$$

$$3 \times 2 = 6 \qquad 3 \times 5 = 15$$

$$3 \times 3 = 9$$

The **least common multiple,** or LCM, of two or more numbers is the common multiple with the lowest value greater than 0. The least common multiple of 2 and 3 is 6.

To compare fractions with unlike denominators, find the LCM of the two denominators. Then, use it to change each fraction to an equivalent fraction with the **least common denominator,** or **LCD.** Say you needed to compare ¾ and ⅚. The two denominators (4 and 6) have an LCM of 12. So change each fraction to an equivalent fraction with a denominator of 12. Then, compare the numerators to see which one is larger.

$$\frac{3 \times 3}{4 \times 3} = \frac{9}{12} \qquad \frac{5 \times 2}{6 \times 2} = \frac{10}{12}$$

$$10 > 9, \text{ so } \frac{10}{12} > \frac{9}{12}, \text{ so } \frac{5}{6} > \frac{3}{4}$$

To compare the values of mixed numbers, first compare the integers. If the integers are the same, then compare the fractions.

$$5\frac{1}{3} > 4\frac{7}{8} \text{ because } 5 > 4.$$

$$6\frac{1}{2} > 6\frac{3}{8} \text{ because } \frac{1}{2} \text{ is greater than } \frac{3}{8}.$$

Adding and Subtracting Fractions

To add fractions with like denominators, add the numerators. The denominator of the sum is the same as the denominator for the two addends.

$$\frac{4}{9} + \frac{3}{9} = \frac{4 + 3}{9} = \frac{7}{9}$$

Juan started doing his homework at 7:00. He spent ¼ of an hour solving math problems and ⅔ of an hour writing a history

report. How much time did Juan spend on his homework? Juan spent ¾ of an hour on his homework.

$$\frac{1}{4} + \frac{2}{4} = \frac{1 + 2}{4} = \frac{3}{4}$$

To subtract fractions with like denominators, subtract the numerators. The denominator of the difference is the same as the denominator for the minuend and subtrahend.

$$\frac{6}{7} - \frac{3}{7} = \frac{6 - 3}{7} = \frac{3}{7}$$

There was ⅚ of an apple pie in the kitchen. Amy and Latoya ate ⅜ of the pie after school. How much pie was left? There was ⅔ of the pie left.

$$\frac{5}{6} - \frac{3}{6} = \frac{5 - 3}{6} = \frac{2}{6}$$

To add or subtract fractions with unlike denominators, you need to find the LCD and convert to equivalent fractions.

Jesse and his father were testing a new fertilizer. A week after being planted, corn plants that had been treated with the new fertilizer grew an average of $^{13}/_{16}$ of an inch. Plants that had not been treated grew an average of $^{2}/_{4}$ of an inch. How much more did the fertilized plants grow during the week?

Write the problem and find the LCD.

$$\frac{13}{16} - \frac{2}{4} =$$

The LCD is 16. Convert $^{2}/_{4}$ to an equivalent fraction with 16 as the denominator

$$\frac{2 \times 4}{4 \times 4} = \frac{8}{16}$$

Subtract the minuend from the subtrahend to find the difference

$$\frac{13}{16} - \frac{2}{4} = \frac{13}{16} - \frac{8}{16} = \frac{5}{16}$$

The corn plants treated with the new fertilizer grew about $^{5}/_{16}$ of an inch more than the plants that were not treated.

The following week, Jesse and his father found that the fertilized corn plants grew another ⅞ of an inch. How much had the fertilized corn grown altogether?

Write the problem and find the LCD.

$$\frac{7}{8} + \frac{13}{16} =$$

The LCD is 16. Convert ⅞ to an equivalent fraction with 16 as the denominator.

$$\frac{7 \times 2}{8 \times 2} = \frac{14}{16}$$

Add the two addends to find the sum.

$$\frac{14}{16} + \frac{13}{16} = \frac{27}{16}$$

The corn treated with fertilizer grew $^{27}/_{16}$ inches altogether.

Sometimes you may want to change improper fractions in your answer to mixed numbers. You may also want to reduce your answer to simplest terms.

For example, $^{27}/_{16}$ is the same as $1^{11}/_{16}$ inches. You could also answer the second problem by saying the corn grew $1^{11}/_{16}$ inches.

Adding Mixed Numbers

To add mixed numbers, add the fraction parts first. Then, add the whole numbers.

Tom collected $2\frac{1}{4}$ pounds of aluminum cans for recycling. Lia collected $3\frac{1}{4}$ pounds of cans. How many pounds did Lia and Tom collect? Lia and Tom collected $5\frac{2}{4}$, or $5\frac{1}{2}$, pounds of cans for recycling.

$$\begin{array}{r} 2\frac{1}{4} \\ +\,3\frac{1}{4} \\ \hline 5\frac{2}{4} \end{array}$$

If the sum of the fraction parts is an improper fraction, change it to a mixed number and add again.

Nikolai collected $3\frac{3}{4}$ pounds of aluminum cans and added them to what Tom and Lia collected. How many pounds did all three of them collect?

$$\begin{array}{r} 2\frac{1}{4} \\ 3\frac{1}{4} \\ +\,3\frac{3}{4} \\ \hline 8\frac{5}{4} \end{array}$$

$\frac{5}{4}$ is an improper fraction. Change it to a mixed number and add it to the integer (8).

$$\frac{5}{4} = 1\frac{1}{4} \qquad 8 + 1\frac{1}{4} = 9\frac{1}{4}$$

Tom, Lia, and Nikolai collected $9\frac{1}{4}$ pounds of cans together.

When adding a mixed number and a whole number, just add the whole numbers. The fraction part of the sum will be the same as the fraction part of the mixed number addend.

$$2 + 1\frac{2}{6} = 3\frac{2}{6}$$

Subtracting Mixed Numbers

To subtract mixed numbers, subtract the fractions first. Then, subtract the whole numbers.

Miguel brought 6⅔ quarts of lemonade to the class picnic. His classmates drank 3⅔ quarts. How much lemonade was left? 3⁰⁄₃ quarts, or 3 quarts, of lemonade were left after the picnic.

$$\begin{array}{r} 6\,{}^{2}/_{3} \\ -\,3\,{}^{2}/_{3} \\ \hline 3\,{}^{0}/_{3} \end{array}$$

Miguel spilled some of the leftover lemonade as he was carrying it back to the bus after the picnic. After the spill, he had 2⅓ quarts left. How much did he spill?

There is no fraction in the minuend from which to subtract the fraction in 2⅓. You need to borrow from the 3. This is like borrowing in the subtraction of whole numbers. When you borrow 1 from the 3, the 3 becomes a 2. Write the 1 that you borrowed as a fraction that has the same denominator as the fraction in the subtrahend. Remember that a fraction in which the numerator and denominator are the same is equal to 1. Write the borrowed 1 as the fraction ³⁄₃ in the minuend. Now, complete the subtraction. Miguel spilled ⅔ of a quart of lemonade.

$$\begin{array}{r} 3 \\ -\,2\,{}^{1}/_{3} \end{array} \qquad 1 = \frac{3}{3} \qquad \begin{array}{r} {}^{2}\!\!\!\!\diagup\!\!3\,{}^{3}/_{3} \\ -\,2\,{}^{1}/_{3} \\ \hline {}^{2}/_{3} \end{array}$$

Multiplying Fractions

Chris helped paint a wall in his school's gymnasium with the school colors. He painted ½ of the wall blue, and he painted ½ of the wall yellow. After the paint dried, he painted ½ of the yellow part of the wall orange. How much of the wall is orange?

part of wall painted yellow —— $\dfrac{1}{2} \times \dfrac{1}{2} = \dfrac{1}{4}$ —— part of whole wall painted orange

part of yellow painted orange

> The word "of" in a word problem often means that you need to multiply. In the example above, "½ of ½" means ½ × ½.

When we multiply fractions, we multiply the numerators to find the numerator for the product, and we multiply the denominators to find the denominator for the product.

Chris started out with ¾ of a gallon of orange paint. He used only ½ of the orange paint on the wall. How much orange paint did he use? Chris used ⅜ of a gallon of orange paint.

$$\frac{3}{4} \times \frac{1}{2} = \frac{3 \times 1}{4 \times 2} = \frac{3}{8}$$

Multiplying Fractions and Whole Numbers

You can use the same rule for multiplying a fraction and a whole number that you use for multiplying fractions.

Every week during the summer, Lewis mows an empty lot for his neighbor, Mrs. Betts. In one hour, Lewis can mow ¼ of the 6-acre lot. How many acres can Lewis mow in one hour?

To find the answer, you must multiply ¼ and 6. To do this, write 6 as a fraction.

$$6 = 6 \div 1 = \frac{6}{1}$$

Now, you can complete the multiplication.

$$\frac{1}{4} \times \frac{6}{1} = \frac{1 \times 6}{4 \times 1} = \frac{6}{4}$$

Convert the answer to a mixed number and reduce it to simplest terms. Lewis can mow 1½ acres in one hour.

$$\frac{6}{4} = 1\frac{2}{4} = 1\frac{1}{2}$$

There is a shortcut for multiplying a fraction and a whole number. Just multiply the numerator in the fraction by the whole number. The denominator for the product will be the same as the denominator in the fraction.

$$\frac{2}{3} \times 8 = \frac{2 \times 8}{3} = \frac{16}{3} = 5\frac{1}{3}$$

Multiplying Mixed Numbers

To multiply mixed numbers, first convert them to fractions. Then, multiply the fractions.

While visiting a state park, Will and Karen walked ½ of a 2½-mile hiking trail, and then they stopped for a picnic lunch. How far had they walked?

It is very important to read and follow directions carefully when working math problems. Sometimes your teacher may ask you to write answers to problems in a certain way, so you may need to change the form of your answer once you have solved a problem.

For example, the instructions may tell you to change improper fractions to mixed numbers or to reduce fractions to their simplest terms. Read and follow instructions carefully so that you can be sure that you have completed every step correctly.

First, write the problem. Then, rewrite the mixed number as a fraction. Then, complete the multiplication and write the answer as a mixed number. Will and Karen walked 1¼ miles.

$$\frac{1}{2} \times 2\frac{1}{2} \qquad 2\frac{1}{2} = \frac{5}{2}$$

$$\frac{1}{2} \times 2\frac{1}{2} = \frac{1}{2} \times \frac{5}{2} = \frac{5}{4} = 1\frac{1}{4}$$

Don't let word problems make you nervous! Follow these steps to solve a word problem:
1. Decide what the problem is asking you to find out.
2. Decide which pieces of information can help you answer the question that the problem is asking.
3. Use the information that you have been given to write a problem.
4. Ask yourself whether the problem you have written will answer the question.
5. Solve the math problem. Don't forget to write your answer in the correct form. For example, the answer to the problem above is not just *1¼*. We were answering the question of how far Will and Karen had walked, so the correct answer is *1¼ miles*.

Dividing with Fractions

Dividing with a fraction is the same as multiplying by the **reciprocal** of the fraction. The reciprocal is the **inverse,** or opposite, of the fraction. The easiest way to divide by a fraction is to **invert and multiply.** This means to turn the fraction upside down by switching the numerator and the denominator.

2 ft

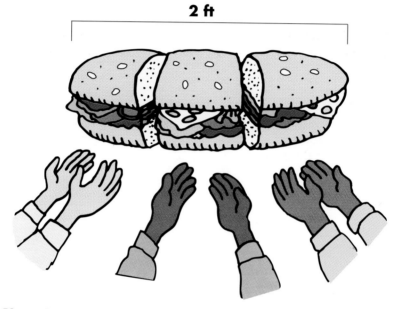

If you have a sandwich that is 2 feet long and you cut it into servings that are ⅔ of a foot each, how many servings will you have?

$$2 \div \frac{2}{3} = 2 \times \frac{3}{2} = \frac{6}{2} = 3$$

The reciprocal rule for dividing by a fraction also applies when you are dividing with improper fractions or with mixed numbers.

$$\frac{2}{3} \div \frac{5}{4} = \frac{2}{3} \times \frac{4}{5} = \frac{8}{15}$$

$$\frac{1}{2} \div 3\frac{1}{4} = \frac{1}{2} \div \frac{13}{4} = \frac{1}{2} \times \frac{4}{13} = \frac{4}{26}$$

Decimals

A Decimal Is . . .

Decimals, like fractions, are used to represent a portion of something. In fact, decimals can be written as fractions called **decimal fractions.** A decimal fraction has a denominator that is 10 or a multiple of 10: $^2/_{10}$, $^{16}/_{100}$, and $^1/_{1,000}$ are all decimal fractions. Most often, though, decimals are written without showing denominators. Decimal numbers have three parts: an **integer;** a **decimal,** which represents an amount between 0 and 1; and a **decimal point,** which separates the integer on the left from the decimal on the right.

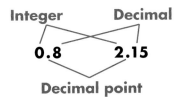

We use the same place value system for decimals that we use for whole numbers. (For information about place values, see pages 5–13.) In a whole number, the value of the place to the right of a digit is always ten times smaller. The tens' place is ten times smaller than the hundreds' place, and the ones' place is ten times smaller than the tens' place.

To find the value of the place to the right of the ones' place, divide one by ten: $1 \div 10 = ^1/_{10}$, or one-tenth. The first place to the right of the decimal point is the **tenths' place.** The value of the place to the right of tenths' place is $^1/_{10} \div 10$, and it is called the **hundredths' place.** The chart on the right shows place values for several decimal places.

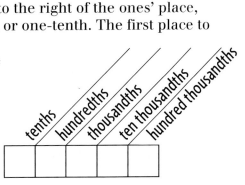

The idea that hundredths have less value than tenths may seem confusing because 100 > 10. Remember that the denominators in fractions like $^1/_{10}$ and $^1/_{100}$ tell how many equal parts something has been divided into. Imagine a pie cut into 100 pieces. Now imagine a pie cut into just 10 pieces. Which pie has bigger pieces? The pie cut into tenths has bigger pieces than the pie divided into hundredths, so we can write $^1/_{10} > ^1/_{100}$.

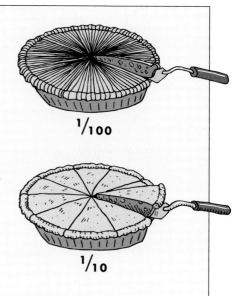

$^1/_{100}$

$^1/_{10}$

Writing Decimal Numbers

Between each whole number, this number line is divided into tenths. Decimals with values less than 1 are written with a 0 in the ones' place. To write *five tenths*, write a 0 in the ones' place and a 5 in the tenths' place, with a decimal point in between: 0.5. Decimals between 1 and 2 have a 1 in the ones' place, decimals between 2 and 3 have a 2 in the ones' place, and so on. Whole numbers can also be written with one or more zeros after the decimal point:
3 = 3.0, 1 = 1.000, 0 = 0.00.

0 0.5 **1**　　**2**　　**3**　　**4**　　**5**

The number line below shows what is in the shaded area on the number line on page 62. Between each of the tenths' values, the number line is divided into hundredths. Notice that the denominator, hundredths, names the last place on the right that is holding a digit.

To write *five hundredths,* write a 0 in the tenths' place and a 5 in the hundredths' place: 0.05. The 0 is needed as a place-holder between the decimal point and the hundredths' digit. For numbers between 0.1 and 0.2, there is a 1 in the tenths' place: 0.11, 0.12, 0.13, and so on. For numbers between 0.2 and 0.3, there is a 2 in the tenths' place, and so on.

How would you write *three and nine hundredths* as a decimal? The *and* tells you where to put the decimal point: after the 3. *Hundredths* tells you that there are two decimal places in the number and that a 9 goes in the hundredths' place.

3.09

Changing Decimals to Fractions

It is easy to convert decimals to fractions. Look at the number 0.27, or twenty-seven hundredths. Hundredths tells you that the denominator is 100. The numerator will be the numeral to the right of the decimal point, which is 27 in this case. Do not write the decimal point in the fraction.

$$0.27 = \frac{27}{100}$$

Changing Fractions to Decimals

It is easy to convert fractions to decimals when the fractions have a denominator that is 10 or a multiple of 10. The denominator will indicate the smallest place value that should appear in the decimal.

$$\frac{5}{10} = 0.5 \qquad\qquad \frac{13}{100} = 0.13$$

$$\frac{8}{100} = 0.08 \qquad\qquad \frac{19}{10} = 1.9$$

You can also change a fraction to a decimal if the fraction has a denominator other than 10 or a multiple of 10, but you need to know about decimal division to do this. See pages 70–71 to learn about decimal division.

Comparing and Ordering Decimals

As with fractions, different decimals can represent the same value. To see that 0.1 = 0.10, write the numbers as fractions and then reduce them to simplest terms:

$$0.1 = \frac{1}{10} \qquad 0.10 = \frac{10}{100} = \frac{1}{10}$$

> For decimals, adding zeros to the *right* of the number *does not* change the value represented by the number. For whole numbers and integers, adding zeros to the *right* of the number *does* change the value represented by the number.
>
> **0.1 = 0.10 but 1 ≠ 10**
>
> Adding zeros to the *left* of a decimal number *does* change the value of the number. Adding zeros to the *left* of whole numbers and integers *does not* change the value of the numbers.
>
> **0.1 ≠ 0.01 but 1 = 01**

To compare decimal numbers, it helps to line up the place values in the numbers. Do that by lining up the decimal points. Then, compare the values of the whole numbers.

12.59
1.9185

12.59 > 1.9185 because 12 > 1

If the whole numbers are equal, compare the decimal place values, starting with the tenths' place. Keep moving to the right across the place values until you find two digits in the same place with different values. In the example below, the digits in the thousandths' place are different.

1.7190
1.7184

1.7190 > 1.7184 because 9 > 8

When comparing whole numbers, you know that the number with more digits is the greater number. However, this is not always true with decimals. A decimal number may have many digits but a very small value.

0.000000786 < 0.1

Estimating Decimals

Sometimes, decimal numbers have many places, and it is easier to work with them if you use estimates. You can use the same methods for estimating decimals that you use for estimating whole numbers. (For information on estimating, see pages 12–13.)

You get different estimates for a number by rounding to different place values. Each of the numbers below is an estimate of 10.0862

10   10.1   10.09   10.086

To round 10.0862 to the nearest hundredth, look at the digit in that place (8). This digit tells you that you will either be rounding down to 10.08 or up to 10.09. To figure out whether to round up or down, look at the digit in the thousandth's place (6). Is 10.086 closer to 10.08 or 10.09? The number line below shows that 10.086 is closer to 10.09, so you round up.

10.08   10.086   10.09

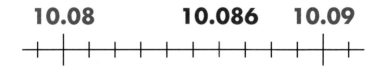

Adding Decimals

Adding decimals is like adding whole numbers. The key to adding decimals is to be sure that the place values in the addends are lined up correctly. The easiest way to do this is to line up the decimal points in the addends.

To add 6.803, 0.01, and 15.98463, make sure the decimal points lie on a straight line. Place a decimal point on the answer line so it is in line with the decimal points in the addends. Now, you can complete the addition. Follow the same rules for regrouping that you use with whole numbers. (For information on regrouping, see pages 17–18.)

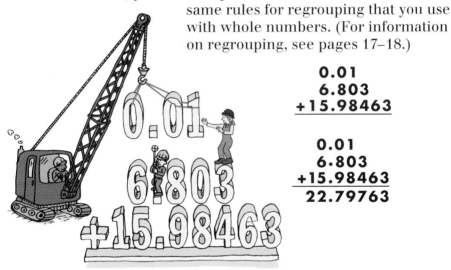

```
   0.01
   6.803
+15.98463
```

```
   0.01
   6.803
+15.98463
 22.79763
```

You may find it helpful to use 0 as a placeholder when adding decimals. Often, you will need to add numbers that do not have the same number of decimal places. You can write more zeros in the addends to the right of the last digit in the decimal so that the addends all have the same number of decimal places.

```
  2.15            2.1500
  4.7             4.7000
  0.5693          0.5693
+31.52         +31.5200
                38.9393
```

Subtracting Decimals

Subtracting decimals is like subtracting whole numbers. The key to subtracting decimals is to make sure the place values in the minuend and subtrahend are lined up correctly. The easiest way to do this is to make sure the decimal points are lined up.

Aisha swam 100 meters in 57.2 seconds at the state swim meet. Her best time for that distance is 55.9 seconds. How much faster was her best performance?

To solve the problem, you need to subtract 55.9 from 57.2. First, line up the decimal points in the minuend and subtrahend. Remember that the difference will have a decimal point. Place it on the answer line so that it is in line with the decimal points in the minuend and subtrahend. Follow the same rules for regrouping that you use in whole-number subtraction. (For information on regrouping, see pages 17–18.)

$$
\begin{array}{r}
57.2 \\
-55.9 \\
\end{array}
\qquad
\begin{array}{r}
6 \\
5\cancel{7}.^{1}2 \\
-55.9 \\
\hline
1.3 \text{ seconds}
\end{array}
$$

Multiplying Decimals

You can multiply decimals by converting them to fractions and then multiplying.

Helen and Trang are measuring the growth of trees in their science class. Helen's tree is 0.8 times as tall as Trang's tree. Trang's tree is 0.9 meters tall. To find how tall Helen's tree is, multiply 0.8 by 0.9 meters.

$$0.8 \times 0.9 = \frac{8}{10} \times \frac{9}{10} = \frac{72}{100} = 0.72 \text{ meters}$$

You can also multiply decimals the same way you multiply whole numbers. The number of decimal places in the product is the sum of the number of decimal places in the factors. Since each factor in the example below has one decimal place, the product has 1 + 1 = 2 decimal places. Count the number of decimal places from the right.

0.9	0.9	0.9	1 decimal place
×0.8	×0.8	×0.8	+1 decimal place
72	72	72	
	000	000	
	072	0.72	2 decimal places

Sometimes a product may have fewer digits than the number of decimal places it needs to have. In the example below, the factors are written without showing the integer part of the number, because its value is 0. The product should have two decimal places, since each factor has one decimal place. Use 0 as a placeholder to show that there are no tenths.

.3	.3	.3
×.2	×.2	×.2
	6	0.06

You can see this by doing the multiplication with decimal fractions:

$$\frac{3}{10} \times \frac{2}{10} = \frac{6}{100} = 0.06$$

Dividing Decimals

When you divide decimal numbers, you use many of the same methods that you use in whole-number division.

Say you want to divide 12.48 by 4. First, write the problem.

$$4\overline{)12.48}$$

When the dividend is a decimal and the divisor is a whole number, the quotient will have a decimal point in the same position as the decimal point in the dividend. Place the decimal point for the quotient before you begin to divide.

$$4\overline{)12.48}^{\bullet}$$

Now, complete the division, following the same rules that you use in long division with whole numbers.

```
      3.12
4)12.48
   -12
     0 4
    - 4
      08
     - 8
       0
```

Sometimes, you may need to add more zeros to the right of the decimal number to complete a division problem. (Remember, adding zeros to the right of a decimal number does not change its value.) You can see this if you divide 8 into 7. You know that there will be no whole number in the quotient because 7 < 8. Write 0 in the quotient above the 7.

```
  0
8)7
```

You can add zeros after the decimal point in the dividend in order to divide. Write a decimal point to the right of the ones' place before adding zeros to the whole-number dividend. Then, finish the division.

```
   0.875
8)7.000
  -64
    60
  - 56
    40
   -40
     0
```

In division problems where both the divisor and the dividend are decimals, you need to change the divisor to a whole number by multiplying it. The number of decimal places in the divisor tells you what you should multiply by to change the divisor to a whole number. If the divisor has one decimal place, multiply by 10 to convert to a whole number. If it has two decimal places, multiply by 100. Then, multiply the dividend by the same number, rewrite the problem, and carry out the division.

$$1.6\overline{)2.56}$$

$$
\begin{array}{r}
1.6 \\
\times\ \ 10 \\
\hline
16.0
\end{array}
\qquad
\begin{array}{r}
2.56 \\
\times\ \ \ 10 \\
\hline
25.60
\end{array}
$$

$$16\overline{)25.6}$$

$$
\begin{array}{r}
1.6 \\
16\overline{)25.6} \\
-16 \\
\hline
96 \\
-96 \\
\hline
0
\end{array}
$$

There is a shortcut for changing decimal divisors to whole numbers. Simply move the decimal point to the right as many places as needed until it is after the ones' place. Then, move the decimal point in the dividend the same number of places.

$$1.25\overline{)2.275} \qquad 1.3\overline{)200.0}$$

Ratios and Proportions

A Ratio Is...

A **ratio** compares two amounts. You can use ratios to compare numbers in different ways. For instance, you can compare part of a set to the whole set. In this set of pets, the ratio of cats to pets is five to eight. The ratio of dogs to pets is three to eight. You can also compare one part of a set to another part. The ratio of cats to dogs is five to three. The ratio of dogs to cats is three to five.

A ratio can be written in three ways.

In words: five to eight

With a symbol: 5:8

As a fraction: $\frac{5}{8}$

Writing Ratios in Simplest Terms

When the numbers in a ratio are large, it can be difficult to see the relationship between them. It often helps to reduce a ratio to its simplest terms. To write a ratio in simplest terms, divide both parts by their **greatest common factor (GCF)**. (For information on reducing to simplest terms with greatest common factors, see pages 45–46.)

The professional basketball season is 82 games long. Reza's favorite team won 60 games and lost 22 games. What is the ratio of wins to losses?

The ratio of wins to losses is 60 to 22, or $^{60}/_{22}$. To write the ratio in simplest terms, divide both parts by their GCF, which is 2.

$$\frac{60}{22} = \frac{60 \div 2}{22 \div 2} = \frac{30}{11}$$

In simplest terms, the ratio is $^{30}/_{11}$. Can you see that this is almost equivalent to $^3/_1$? Reza's team won almost three times as many games as they lost.

Reducing a ratio to simplest terms does not change the relationship between the numbers. The ratio of balls to blocks is 4:6. Notice that there are two balls for every three blocks. We can reduce the ratio 4:6 to 2:3.

A Proportion Is ...

A **proportion** is a number statement that says that two ratios are equal.

$$\frac{3}{4} = \frac{6}{8}$$

The ratios in a proportion are usually written in the form of fractions. Did you notice that the two ratios in the example above are equivalent fractions? Remember that equivalent fractions represent the same value.

Ratios and proportions are used to make many kinds of information easier to understand or use. For example, proportions are used to figure out how to represent distances on maps and atlases. On a road map, the distances between points are **proportional** to the actual driving distances. In other words, distances on the map are related to one another in the same way that the actual distances are related. If one town is exactly twice as far away as another town, a map will show them to be exactly twice as far away, too, but on a smaller scale.

The **scale** of a map, or its relationship to actual distances, is shown in the map's legend.

Whitesville is 5 miles from Reynolds Station and 10 miles from Fordsville. On a map, Whitesville and Reynolds Station are 1 inch apart, and Whitesville and Fordsville are 2 inches apart. Another way to say this is that $^5/_{10} = ^1/_2$. The legend shows that 1 inch = 5 miles, so 2 inches = 10 miles.

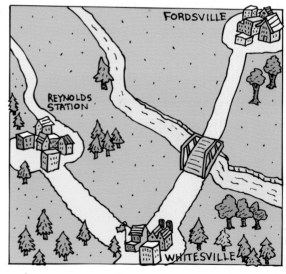

5 Miles

Checking Proportions

When working with proportions, it is very important to check your work. To check a proportion, divide or multiply both parts of one ratio by the same number. The goal is to get an answer that is the same as the second ratio in the proportion.

James is building models of the tallest buildings in the United States. The Empire State Building is about 1,250 feet tall, and it has a tower on top that is about 200 feet tall. James's model is 25 inches tall, with a tower 4 inches tall. Are the proportions correct?

First, write the proportion as stated in the problem:

$$\frac{4}{25} = \frac{200}{1,250}$$

Can you think of a number to multiply by 4 to get a product of 200? That number is 50. If you multiply both parts of the first ratio by 50, you'll see that James's proportions are correct.

$$\frac{4}{25} = \frac{4 \times 50}{25 \times 50} = \frac{200}{1,250}$$

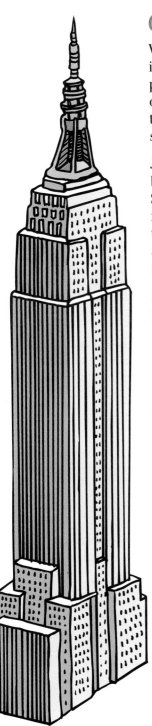

Another way to check proportions is to use **cross products.** To find a cross product, multiply each numeral in the first ratio by the numeral that is *diagonally across* from it. The two products should be the same.

$$\frac{4}{25} \diagup\!\!\!\!\!\diagdown \frac{200}{1,250} \qquad \begin{matrix} 4 \times 1{,}250 = 5{,}000 \\ 25 \times 200 = 5{,}000 \end{matrix}$$

You can use cross products to find a missing value in a proportion.

Now James is working on a model of the Sears Tower. The Empire State Building is about 1,250 feet tall, and James's model is 25 inches tall. The Sears Tower is about 1,450 feet tall. How tall should the model of the Sears Tower be?

Write the problem as a proportion. Then find the cross products.

$$\frac{25}{1,250} = \frac{\textbf{height of Sears Tower model}}{1,450}$$

$$25 \times 1{,}450 = \text{height of model} \times 1{,}250$$

$$36{,}250 = \text{height of model} \times 1{,}250$$

This last equation doesn't tell you what "height of model" equals, but it does tell you what "height of model" times 1,250 equals: 36,250. To find the height of the model, divide both sides of the equation by 1,250. On the left side of the equals sign, you'll end up with a number: 36,250 ÷ 1,250. On the right side of the equals sign, you'll end up with just "height of model." The equation will still be correct because you made the same change (dividing by 1,250) on *both sides of the equals sign.* (For more information on these kinds of problems, see pages 116–117.)

$$\frac{36{,}250}{1,250} = \frac{\text{height of model} \times 1{,}250}{1,250}$$

$$29 = \text{height of model}$$

The model of the Sears Tower should be 29 inches tall.

Percents

A Percent Is . . .

Like fractions and decimals, **percents** are a way of representing part of something.

Let's say your school auditorium has 100 seats, and you've sold tickets for 72 of them for your upcoming class play. Think of different ways you can show how many tickets have been sold.

Use a fraction: $\frac{72}{100}$

Use a decimal: 0.72

You can also use a percent to represent the number of tickets sold. Percent means "for every hundred" or "out of a hundred." 72 of the 100 seats, or 72 **percent**, have been sold. Often, you will see the symbol % used in place of the word *percent*. 72 percent = 72%

Changing Decimals and Fractions to Percents

To change a decimal to a percent, move the decimal point two places to the right.

1.56   1.56   156 percent (156%)

Sometimes, you will need to use 0 as a placeholder digit when changing decimals to percents.

0.5   0.50   50 percent (50%)

To change a fraction to a percent, change the fraction to a decimal. First, divide the numerator by the denominator. Add zeros to the dividend if necessary. Then write the decimal as a percent.

$$\frac{4}{5} \qquad 5)\overline{4.0} \;\; 0.8$$

```
       0.8
   5)4.0
     -0
      40
    - 40
       0
```

0.8   0.80   80 percent (80%) $\frac{4}{5}$ = 80 percent

Changing Percents to Decimals and Fractions

To change a percent to a decimal, just move the decimal point two places to the left. Remember that the decimal point in a whole number is to the right of the ones' place, even though it is not written.

72%   72.
          move
          decimal

0.72
write in
decimal form

Once the percent is in decimal form, it is easy to change it to a fraction. Just use the decimal as the numerator of a fraction with 100 as the denominator, and then simplify if necessary.

$$72\% = 0.72 = \frac{72}{100} = \frac{18}{25}$$

Sometimes you will need to add more zeros to the left of a numeral when changing from a percent to a decimal.

6%   06.   0.06

Finding Percents

Percents are used to express many different kinds of relationships. They can be used to represent the number of people
who voted in an election, the amount of change in the price
of something, or the chance that
some event—like rainfall or snow-
fall—will happen.

In a recent election, 77 percent of the
registered voters in Littleton cast bal-
lots. There are 13,500 registered voters
in Littleton. How many people voted
in the election? To solve the problem,
you must multiply the number of registered voters (13,500) by the percent
who voted (77%). First, change the
percent to a decimal. Then, complete
the multiplication. Remember to
place a decimal point in the product.

$$
\begin{array}{r}
13,500 \\
\times \quad 77\% \\
\end{array}
$$

$$77\% = 0.77$$

$$
\begin{array}{r}
13,500 \\
\times \quad 0.77 \\
\hline
94500 \\
+945000 \\
\hline
10,395.00 \\
\end{array}
$$

10,395 people voted in the election.

What percent of the registered voters in Littleton did not vote
in the election? How many registered voters did not vote?

The number of registered voters who did not vote is equal to
the total number of registered voters minus the number of
registered voters who voted. $100\% - 77\% = 23\%$, so 23 percent of the registered voters did not vote. $23\% \times 13,500 =$
$0.23 \times 13,500 = 3,105$, so 3,105 registered voters did not vote.

Using Percents to Solve Problems

Percents are often used to make numbers more meaningful. For example, the fact that 10 of your classmates prefer musical comedies and 15 of them prefer serious dramas means more when you know the total number of your classmates. If you have only 25 classmates, you know that they all prefer musical comedies or serious dramas. If you have 100 classmates, you know that most of them prefer other kinds of films. Percents are useful in expressing these kinds of relationships.

Mrs. Branley teaches music classes at Pulaski Elementary School. She told her students that they could go to either a symphony concert or a performance of the musical *Cats* on the annual field trip. There are 125 students in Mrs. Branley's classes. 70 students voted to see *Cats*. To find what percent of the students voted to see *Cats*, you must divide the number who voted to see *Cats* (70) by the total number of students (125).

$$
\begin{array}{r}
0.56 \\
125\overline{)70.00} \\
-0 \\
\hline
700 \\
-625 \\
\hline
750 \\
-750 \\
\hline
0
\end{array}
$$

56 percent of the students voted to see *Cats*.

How many students voted to attend the symphony concert? You can find this number in two ways:

By subtracting actual numbers
125 – 70 = 55 students

Or by subtracting using percents, and multiplying by the total number of students
100% – 56% = 44%
44% × 125 = 0.44 × 125 = 55 students

Measurement

Measurement Is...

When you **measure** something, you describe one of its properties by using a **scale** made up of **units**. All of the units on the scale are the same size. You can measure many different properties of an object: length, height, distance, weight, volume, temperature, time, and so on.

Measuring helps you to compare things. When you want to know who ran the fastest in a close race, you can compare the times of the runners. When you want to know who jumped the farthest, you can measure and compare the lengths of jumps by different people.

Measuring also allows you to describe things in ways that others can easily understand. To share your cookie recipe with someone, you would give measurements for all of the ingredients. If you were going to visit a friend, you could agree on a time so that it would be easier to plan the visit.

Quick Cookies
1 cup peanut butter
1 cup brown sugar
1 egg
4 tablespoons Chocolate Chips

Systems of Measurement

If you use an object—the width of your hand, for example—to measure the length or height of something, your hand is the **unit of measure**. A **standard unit of measure** is one that everyone has agreed to use.

In a system of measurement, all of the units are related in some way. You probably know that 12 inches make up 1 foot and that 3 feet make up 1 yard. For a system of measurement to work, people must agree on it. In the system used in the United States, for instance, all measures of length can be related to the inch. If an inch didn't mean the same thing to two people, it would be hard to even talk about the length of an object.

The two most common systems of measurement are the **customary system** and the **metric system**. In the United States, we use the customary system, but almost all other countries use the metric system. The metric system is a **decimal system**: The smaller units are grouped by tens to form the larger units.

Customary System

Length

Unit	Abbreviation	Equivalent	Metric Conversion
mile	mi	5,280 feet	1.61 kilometers
rod	rd	16.5 feet	5.03 meters
yard	yd	3 feet or 36 inches	0.91 meter
foot	ft	12 inches	30.48 centimeters
inch	in	0.083 foot	2.54 centimeters

Area

Unit	Abbreviation	Equivalent	Metric Conversion
square mile	sq mi	640 acres	2.59 square kilometers
acre		43,560 square feet	4,047 square meters
square rod	sq rd	272.25 square feet	25.29 square meters
square yard	sq yd	9 square feet	0.84 square meter
square foot	sq ft	144 square inches	0.093 square meter
square inch	sq in	0.0069 square foot	6.45 square centimeters

Volume

Unit	Abbreviation	Equivalent	Metric Conversion
cubic yard	cu yd	27 cubic feet	0.76 cubic meter
cubic foot	cu ft	1,728 cubic inches	0.028 cubic meter
cubic inch	cu in	0.00058 cubic foot	16.39 cubic centimeters

Liquid Measure

Unit	Abbreviation	Equivalent	Metric Conversion
barrel	bar	31.5 gallons	119.7 liters
gallon	ga	4 quarts	3.8 liters
quart	qt	2 pints	0.95 liter
pint	pt	4 gills or 16 fluid ounces	0.47 liter
gill	gi	4 fluid ounces	118.4 milliliters
fluid ounce	fl oz	0.0078 gallon	29.6 milliliters

Weight

Unit	Abbreviation	Equivalent	Metric Conversion
short ton		2,000 pounds	0.91 metric ton
short hundredweight		100 pounds	45.36 kilograms
long ton		2,240 pounds	1.016 metric tons
long hundredweight		112 pounds	50.8 kilograms
pound	lb	16 ounces	0.45 kilogram
ounce	oz	16 drams or 0.0625 pound	28.35 grams
dram	dr	27.344 grains or 0.0625 ounce	1.77 grams
grains	gr	0.037 dram or 0.00229 ounce	0.065 gram

METRIC SYSTEM

Length

Unit	Abbreviation	Equivalent	Customary Conversion
kilometer	km	1,000 meters	0.62 mile
hectometer	hm	100 meters	328 feet
dekameter	dam	10 meters	32.81 feet
meter	m	1 meter	39.37 inches
decimeter	dm	0.1 meter	3.94 inches
centimeter	cm	0.01 meter	0.39 inch
millimeter	mm	0.001 meter	0.039 inch

Area

Unit	Abbreviation	Equivalent	Customary Conversion
square kilometer	sq km	1,000,000 square meters	0.39 square mile
hectare	ha	10,000 square meters	2.47 acres
are	a	100 square meters	119.6 square yards
square meter	sq m	1 square meter	10.75 square feet
square centimeter	sq cm	0.0001 square meter	0.15 square inch

Volume

Unit	Abbreviation	Equivalent	Customary Conversion
cubic meter	m³	1 cubic meter	1.31 cubic yards
cubic decimeter	dm³	0.001 cubic meter	61 cubic inches
cubic centimeter	cm³	0.000001 cubic meter	0.061 cubic inch

Liquid Measure

Unit	Abbreviation	Equivalent	Customary Conversion
dekaliter	dal	10 liters	2.64 gallons
liter	l	1 liter	1.06 quarts
deciliter	dl	0.1 liter	0.21 pint
centiliter	cl	0.01 liter	0.34 fluid ounce
milliliter	ml	0.001 liter	0.034 fluid ounce

Weight

Unit	Abbreviation	Equivalent	Customary Conversion
metric ton	t	1,000,000 grams	1.102 short tons
kilogram	kg	1,000 grams	2.2 pounds
hectogram	hg	100 grams	3.53 ounces
dekagram	dag	10 grams	0.35 ounce
gram	g	1 gram	0.035 ounce
decigram	dg	0.1 gram	1.55 grains
centigram	cg	0.01 gram	0.15 grain
milligram	mg	0.001 gram	0.015 grain

Converting Units

The key to changing from one unit to another is to know how they are related. The charts on pages 82–87 show the numbers you need to know to convert one unit to another. The numbers that you divide or multiply by are called **conversion factors**. You can use conversion factors to convert measurements within a system; for example, you can convert feet to inches. You can also use them to convert measurements from one system to another; for example, you can convert pounds to kilograms.

Wesley is 60 inches tall. What is his height in feet?

There are 12 inches in a foot, so the number of feet needed to tell Wesley's height will be less than the number of inches. If you divide the number of inches by 12, you'll find that Wesley is 5 feet tall.

60 ÷ 12 = 5   5 feet = 60 inches

Gina needs a board that is 6 feet long on which to build her model railroad. The lumber yard sells the kind of board she needs by the inch. How many inches of board does Gina need?

It will take a greater number of inches to represent the same length as 6 feet. If you multiply 6 by the number of inches in a foot, you'll find that Gina needs a board that is 72 inches long.

6 x 12 = 72   6 feet = 72 inches

Sometimes you will need to solve problems involving measurements made with different units. To do this, you need to find common units for the measurements.

Annie and Monica each knitted a scarf. Annie's is 57 inches long. Monica's is 5 feet long. How much longer is Monica's scarf?

Convert Monica's measurement to inches, and then subtract to find the difference between the length of the scarves. You'll find that Monica's scarf is 3 inches longer.

5 x 12 = 60 inches   60 – 57 = 3 inches

Remember, if you are converting to smaller units, multiply by the conversion factor; if you are converting to larger units, divide by the conversion factor.

Choosing Units Wisely

You need to choose a unit that is the right size for what you are measuring. For example, you would not use the same unit of weight for an ant that you would use for an elephant. When choosing units of measure, use your common sense to pick a unit that is the right size.

What unit of length or distance would you use to measure (1) the cord on a set of headphones, (2) a hallway in your school, and (3) the distance between New York and Los Angeles?

You could easily measure the length of the cord on a set of headphones in inches or centimeters. To measure a hallway in your school, you would want a larger unit—feet or meters. For long distances, such as those between cities, miles or kilometers are the best units to use.

Measuring Time

We use hours, minutes, and seconds to measure time. The 12 numbers on a clock represent the hours in a day. There are 24 hours in 1 day, so the hour (short) hand on a clock goes around twice in a day. Midnight (12:00 A.M.) marks the end of one day and the beginning of the next.

There are 60 minutes in 1 hour, which is the time it takes for the minute (long) hand to go around the clock once. The space between each numeral represents five minutes. Minutes are often marked on a clock with hash marks between the numerals.

We tell time by stating the hour followed by the number of minutes past the hour. You can tell the number of minutes quickly by counting by fives. **A.M.** stands for *ante meridiem,* or "before the middle of the day"; it is used for the hours between midnight and noon. **P.M.** stands for *post meridiem,* or "after the middle of the day"; it is used for the hours between noon and midnight.

You can write times with numerals or words.

2:24

Two twenty-four

When the minute hand is past the 30-minute mark, you can say the time is "____ minutes 'til the next hour."

1:40

One forty

Twenty minutes 'til two.

For 15 minutes past the hour, you can use the expression "a quarter past" or "a quarter after." For 30 minutes past the hour, you can use the expression "half past." For 45 minutes past the hour, you can use the expression "a quarter 'til."

Calculating Elapsed Time

Sometimes you will need to know the amount of time that has passed.

On Saturdays, Edyta takes a train to visit her grandmother. The train leaves Chicago at 7:13 and stops near her grandmother's home at 8:20. How long is Edyta's train ride?

To solve the problem, subtract the earlier time from the later time. The ride takes 1 hour and 7 minutes.

$$
\begin{array}{r}
\text{8 hours 20 minutes} \\
-\text{ 7 hours 13 minutes} \\
\hline
\text{1 hour \quad 7 minutes}
\end{array}
$$

Sometimes Edyta meets her grandmother for breakfast at her favorite restaurant. The train stops near the restaurant at 8:05. How long is Edyta's ride then?

You have to borrow 1 hour from the hours in the minuend in order to be able to subtract the minutes. Add 60 minutes to the minutes in the minuend and complete the subtraction. The ride takes 52 minutes.

$$
\begin{array}{r}
\text{8 hr \quad 5 min} \\
-\text{ 7 hr 13 min} \\
\end{array}
$$

$$
\begin{array}{r}
^{7} \\
\cancel{8}\text{ hr 65 min} \\
-\text{ 7 hr 13 min} \\
\hline
\text{52 min}
\end{array}
$$

Money

Denominations of Money

The money system of the United States is based on the system of decimal numbers. The basic unit of American money is the dollar.

Denominations, or values, of money worth one dollar or more come in the form of paper money called **bills.** People commonly use bills of different denominations, such as one dollar, five dollars, ten dollars, twenty dolars, fifty dollars, and one hundred dollars. Denominations of less than a dollar are in units called **cents.** One cent is worth ¹⁄₁₀₀ of a dollar.

100 cents = 1 dollar

The symbol $ is used to show that a numeral represents an amount of American money. If there are no cents, an amount of money may be written as a whole number. Amounts that include cents are written as decimal numbers to the hundredths' place. A decimal point separates the number of dollars from the number of cents.

$10.00   ten dollars

$1.06   one dollar and six cents

$80.14   eighty dollars and fourteen cents

If the amount of money is less than one dollar, you can write the amount with a dollar sign or with the cents sign (¢). You do not use a decimal point when you use ¢.

$.75   **$.05**   **$.99**

75¢   **5¢**   **99¢**

Coins and Their Value	Number of coins needed to make $1
1 penny = 1 cent = 0.01 dollar or $0.01	100
1 nickel = 5 cents = 0.05 dollar or $0.05	20
1 dime = 10 cents = 0.10 dollar or $0.10	10
1 quarter = 25 cents = 0.25 dollar or $0.25	4
1 half-dollar = 50 cents = 0.50 dollar or $0.50	2

You can add, subtract, multiply, and divide amounts of money just as you can other numbers. You can solve problems involving money the same way you solve other decimal number problems. (For information on problems with decimal numbers, see pages 61–71.)

Geometry

Geometry Is...

Geometry deals with relationships between points, lines, angles, surfaces, and solids.

A **point** is a position in space. Although a dot may be used to represent a point in a sketch or diagram, a real point has no size or shape; it is just a location. In geometry, we use capital letters to name points.

A **line** is made up of points. A line goes on and on in opposite directions. You can name a line by naming any two points on the line. A line has length but no width, but we often represent lines by sketching them with a pencil.

This is the line XY.

A **plane** is a flat surface that goes on and on in all directions. You can name a plane by naming any three points in the plane.

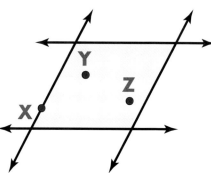

This is the plane XYZ.

A **line segment** is part of a line. A line goes on and on in opposite directions, but a line segment has two **endpoints.** You name a line segment by naming its two endpoints.

This is the line segment XY.

A **ray** is also part of a line. It has an endpoint at one end but goes on and on in the opposite direction. You name a ray by naming its endpoint and one other point on the ray.

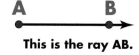

This is the ray AB.

Relationships Between Lines

Lines, line segments, and rays may be related to each other in several ways.

Intersecting lines are two lines that cross at some point.

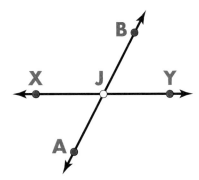

XY intersects AB at point J.

An **angle** is formed by two rays that share an endpoint. The shared endpoint is called the **vertex** of the angle. Name an angle by naming one point on each ray, with the vertex in the middle.

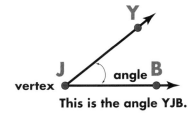

This is the angle YJB.

Perpendicular lines are two lines that intersect and form right angles, or angles of 90°.(See page 96 for more information about right angles.) The symbol ⊥ means "is perpendicular to."

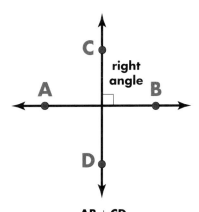

AB ⊥ CD
Read "AB is perpendicular to CD."

Parallel lines are lines in the same plane that never intersect. The symbol ‖ means "is parallel to."

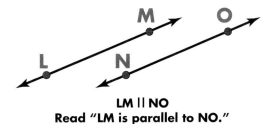

LM ‖ NO
Read "LM is parallel to NO."

Angles

Angles are an important part of geometry. The unit of measure for angles is the **degree,** which is represented by the symbol °.

You can measure angles with a **protractor.** Place the center of the protractor on the vertex of the angle and line up the flat side of the protractor with one of the rays that form the angle. Look at where the other ray crosses the round edge of the protractor. The number on the scale of the protractor where the ray crosses tells you the measure of the angle in degrees.

An angle with a measure of 90° is called a **right angle.** Two lines that form a right angle are called **perpendicular lines.**

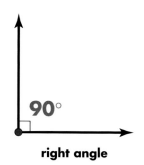

90°

right angle

An angle with a measure between 0° and 90° is called an **acute** angle.

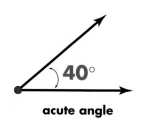

40°

acute angle

An angle with a measure between 90° and 180° is called an **obtuse** angle.

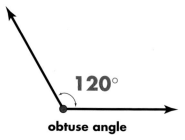

120°

obtuse angle

You can also use a protractor to draw angles. Draw three points: one at the center of the protractor, one at 0°, and one at the measure you want. Then, draw rays connecting the vertex to the other points.

Most protractors have two scales printed on them, an **inner** scale and an **outer** scale. If the ray along the straight edge of the protractor runs *to the right*, read the angle measure from the inner scale. If the ray along the straight edge runs *to the left*, read the angle measure from the outer scale.

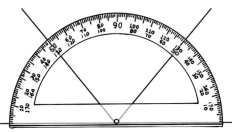

Two angles whose sum is 90° are called **complementary angles.** Angles BAC and DAC are complementary angles. Two angles whose sum is 180° are called **supplementary angles.** Angles RST and UST are supplementary angles.

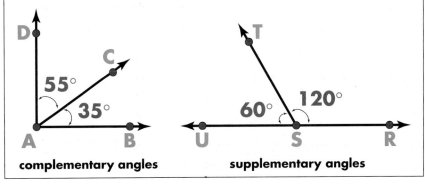

complementary angles   supplementary angles

Polygons

A **polygon** is a closed figure made up of line segments that are in the same plane. The line segments make up the sides of the polygon. The point where two sides meet is called a **vertex**.

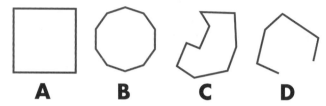

A   B   C   D

Are all of the above figures polygons? Figure D is not a polygon because it is not a closed figure.

Polygons are described according to the number of sides or angles they have. The number of angles and the number of sides are the same. The chart below shows examples of some different kinds of polygons.

	triangle	3 sides	3 angles
	quadrilateral	4 sides	4 angles
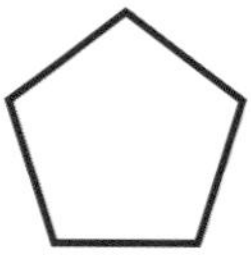	pentagon	5 sides	5 angles
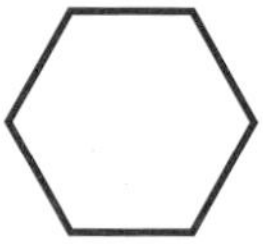	hexagon	6 sides	6 angles
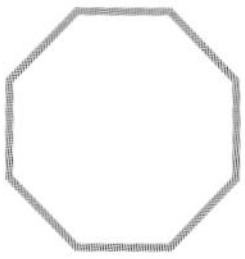	octagon	8 sides	8 angles

A **regular polygon** has sides that are all of equal length. The angles in a regular polygon are also equal.

Congruent polygons are polygons that have the same size and shape. Corresponding (matching) sides and angles are equal in congruent polygons. In these congruent triangles, corresponding sides and angles are equal.

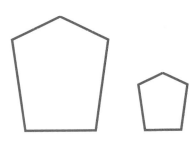 **Similar polygons** have the same shape but do not have to be the same size. Corresponding angles in similar polygons are equal, but corresponding sides may differ in length. The ratios of corresponding sides in similar polygons are always equal.

Symmetric polygons are polygons that can be divided into two congruent parts. One side is the mirror image of the other. A symmetric polygon may have one or more **lines of symmetry** that divide it into two congruent parts.

Not all figures have lines of symmetry.

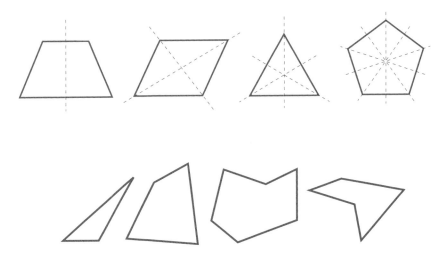

Quadrilaterals

A **quadrilateral** is a polygon with four sides and four angles.

Several kinds of quadrilaterals have special names.

A **trapezoid** is a quadrilateral with exactly one pair of opposite sides that are parallel. In the trapezoids below, AB ‖ CD and WX ‖ YZ.

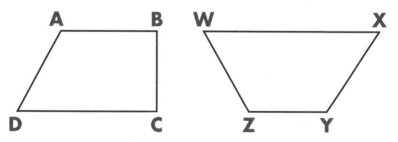

A **parallelogram** is a quadrilateral with opposite sides that are parallel. Opposite sides in a parallelogram are also congruent. (The symbol ≅ means "is congruent to.") In the parallelogram below, AB ‖ CD and AB ≅ CD; AD ‖ BC and AD ≅ BC.

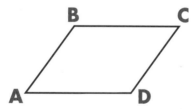

A **rhombus** is a special kind of parallelogram: All of its sides are congruent. In the rhombus below, AB ‖ CD, AD ‖ BC, and AB ≅ CD ≅ AD ≅ BC.

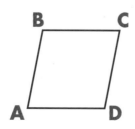

A **rectangle** is a special kind of parallelogram: All four of
its angles are right angles. In the rectangle below, ∠ ABC,
∠ BCD, ∠ CDA, and ∠ DAB are all right angles. Because they
have the same measure, they are congruent.

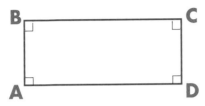

A **square** is a special kind of rectangle: All four of its sides are
congruent. A square is also a special kind of rhombus: All four
of its angles are right angles.

In the square below, AB ≅ CD ≅ AD ≅ BC. Hash marks on the
sides of the figure show that they are congruent.

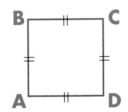

The features that tell us what a geometric figure is are called its **defining features.** Defining features are
very important in geometry because
they tell you how figures are alike
and different. For example, all
squares are rectangles, but not all
rectangles are squares. To understand why this is true, compare the
definitions of the two. A rectangle
and a square both have four right
angles. A square must also have four
congruent sides, but not all rectangles have four congruent sides.

Triangles

A **triangle** is a polygon with three sides and three angles. All of the figures below are triangles.

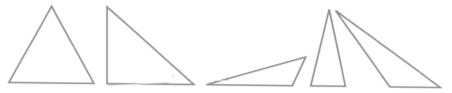

Several kinds of triangles have special names. They are named for their angle measures or the lengths of their sides.

An **equilateral triangle** has three sides of congruent length.

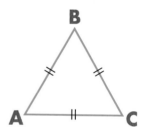

An **isosceles triangle** has two congruent sides.

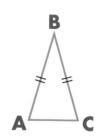

A **scalene triangle** has sides that are all different lengths.

A **right triangle** has one right angle.

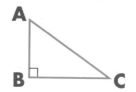

An **obtuse triangle** has one obtuse angle.

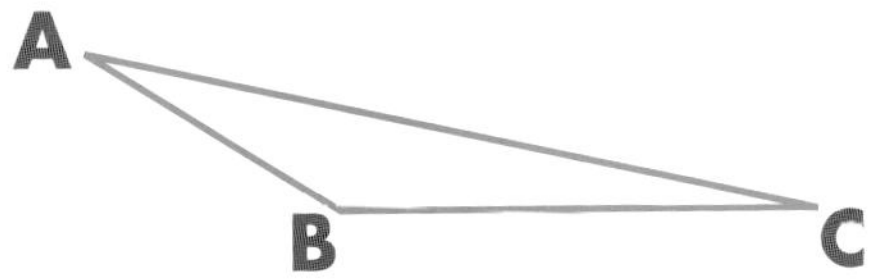

The angles of an **acute triangle** are all acute.

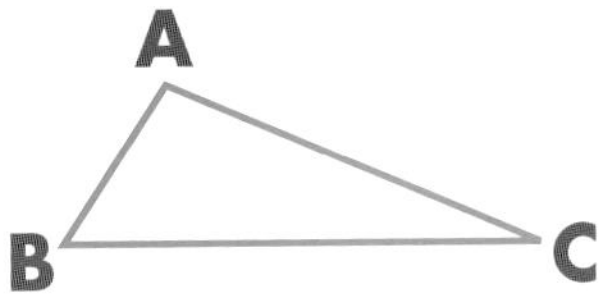

A triangle can have more than one name. For example, an isosceles triangle can also be a right triangle, and a scalene triangle can also be an obtuse triangle.

Circles

A **circle** is a figure with all points the same distance from a point called the **center.** A circle is named by the point at its center.

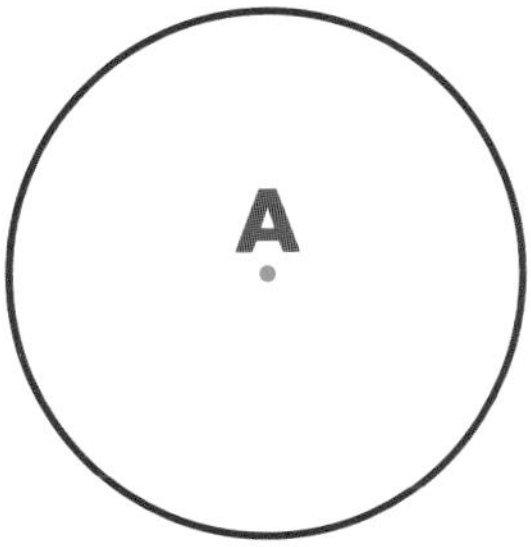

This is circle A.

A **radius** is a line segment with one endpoint on the circle and the other endpoint at the center. A **diameter** is a line segment that passes through the center of the circle and has both endpoints on the circle. A diameter of a circle is twice as long as its radius. A **chord** is a line segment with

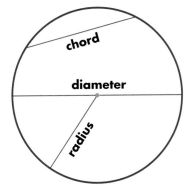

both endpoints on the circle. A
diameter is a special type of chord.
An **arc** is the part of a circle that is
between the endpoints of a chord. A
semicircle is half of a circle. A
semicircle is a special kind of arc.

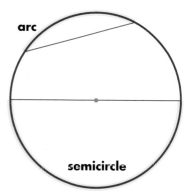

If you know the length of the radius, it is
easy to find the length of the diameter. The
diameter is twice as long as the radius, so
multiply the radius by 2 to find the length of
the diameter. If you know the length of the
diameter, divide it by 2 to find the length of
the radius.

You can use a drawing tool called a compass
to make a circle. Set the metal point where
you want the center of the circle. Use the
scale on the compass to set the length of the
radius. Hold the compass at the top and rotate
the pencil around the metal point to draw the
circle.

Graphing Ordered Pairs

When solving geometry problems, you will find it helpful to
make sketches or graphs of figures. You can use graph paper
to make sketches that represent lines and figures. Graph
paper is printed with a pattern of squares called a **grid.** To
locate points on the grid, you can use two numbers called an
ordered pair. To make a figure, you can draw lines connecting points on a graph.

Look at the graph shown here. The horizontal number line is called the **x-axis,** and the vertical number line is called the **y-axis.** The ordered pair (3,4) locates point A on the graph. To find the first number in the ordered pair for point A, start at the origin (0) on the x-axis and count three spaces to the right. To find the second number in the ordered pair, start at the origin on the y-axis and count up four spaces.

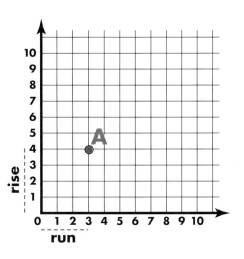

The distance on the x-axis (3) is called the **run** or the **x-coordinate**; the distance on the y-axis (4) is called the **rise** or the **y-coordinate.** In an ordered pair, the x-coordinate is always listed first. The y-coordinate is the second number in an ordered pair.

Finding Perimeter

Perimeter is the distance around a polygon. To find the perimeter of a polygon, add the lengths of its sides.

Mr. Evans plans to put a fence around his garden. How much fencing will he need to buy? To find the perimeter of Mr. Evans's garden, add the lengths of its sides.

Perimeter = 14 + 14 + 18 + 18 = 64 feet

Mr. Evans will need to buy 64 feet of fencing material.

In some cases, you do not need to know the lengths of all of the sides to find the perimeter. For example, you only need to know the length of one side of a square or rhombus to find the perimeter because all sides of a square are congruent.

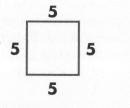

perimeter = 4 × 5 = 20

Perimeter of a square = 4 × (length of side) or P = 4s

To find the perimeter of a parallelogram or rectangle, you need to know the length of two sides, since the opposite sides will be of the same length.

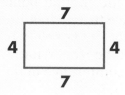

**Perimeter = (2 × 7) + (2 × 4)
= 14 + 8 = 22**

Perimeter of parallelogram = (2 × length) + (2 × width) or P = 2l + 2w

To find the perimeter of an equilateral triangle, you only need to know the length of one side because all of the sides are congruent.

perimeter = 3 × 4 = 12

Perimeter of equilateral triangle = 3 × (length of side) or P = 3s

Circumference

Circumference is the term used for the perimeter of a circle. To find the circumference of a circle, you need to use a special formula:

$$C = \pi \times d$$

C stands for circumference and d stands for the length of the diameter, a line segment with both endpoints on the circle that passes through the center of the circle. The Greek letter *pi (π)* represents the ratio of the circumference of the circle to its diameter. This ratio has the same value for every circle, no matter what size. The value of π is about 3.14159.

Kenneth wants to build a bench around a large oak tree in his yard. The diameter of the circular bench will have to be 8 feet in order for the bench to fit around the tree. What will the circumference of the bench be?

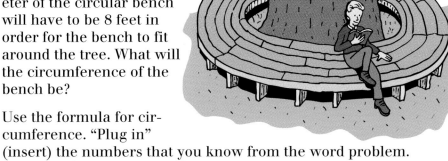

Use the formula for circumference. "Plug in" (insert) the numbers that you know from the word problem. Use 3.14159 as the value of π.

$$C = π × d = 3.14159 × 8 = 25.13272$$

The circumference of Kenneth's bench will be about 25.13 feet, or about 25 feet and 1½ inches.

Area of a Rectangle

The space taken up by a flat surface is called its **area.**

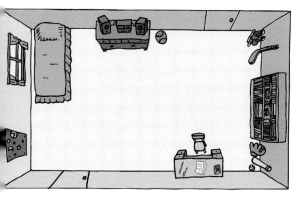

Tim is going to get new carpet in his bedroom. He has to figure out how much carpet he needs to cover the floor. To solve this problem, he needs to know the area of the bedroom floor, or the amount of space the floor takes up.

You can use a unit of measure called a **square foot** to find the area of Tim's room. A square foot represents a square with sides that are 1 foot long. To find the area of Tim's room, find out how many square feet fit in the floor space of the room. Count the squares in the diagram. There are 240 squares, which means that the area of the room is

1 foot

1 foot

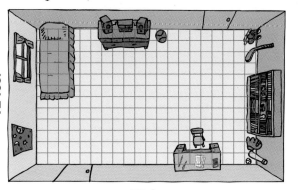

12 feet

20 feet

240 square feet. You can also find the number of square feet by multiplying the length of the room by the width.

12 feet × 20 feet = 240 square feet

> Some units used to measure area include the square inch, square centimeter, square yard, square meter, square mile, and so on.

Finding Areas of Regular Shapes

Formulas make it easy to find the areas of regular shapes. To find the area of a square or rectangle, for example, multiply the length by the width.

4 in.

4 in.

5 cm

8 cm

A = l × w =
4 × 4 = 16 square inches

A = l × w =
8 × 5 = 40 square centimeters

To find the area of a parallelo-gram, multiply the length of the base by the height of the figure.

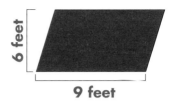

6 feet

9 feet

$$A = l \times h = 9 \times 6 = 54 \text{ square feet}$$

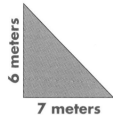

6 meters

7 meters

To find the area of a triangle, multiply the height by ½ the length of the base. This formula treats a triangle as if it is one half of a parallelogram.

$$A = \tfrac{1}{2}b \times h = \tfrac{1}{2}(7) \times 6 = \tfrac{7}{2} \times 6 = \tfrac{42}{2} = 21 \text{ square meters}$$

To find the area of a circle, use the for-mula $A = \pi r^2$. (r^2 means $r \times r$, and you read it as "r squared.")

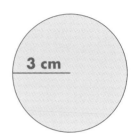

3 cm

$$A = \pi r^2 = 3.14159 \times 3 \times 3 = 3.14159 \times 9 = 28.27431 \text{ square centimeters}$$

Formulas often use letters to stand for words. This makes it easier to write and to remember the formulas. Here is a list of letters commonly used in geometric formulas:
A = area
C = circumference
P = perimeter
V = volume
b = base
d = diameter
h = height
l = length
r = radius
w = width

Finding Surface Area

A **space figure** is a figure that represents an object that can be filled. For example, a cup can hold water or some other liquid. The cup shown here is a space figure.

One important feature of a space figure is its **surface area,** which is the combined area of all of its sides. Another important feature is its **volume** or **capacity.** This tells us how much it will hold.

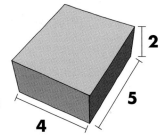

This space figure represents a rectangular prism. All of the **faces,** or sides, of a rectangular prism are rectangles. The prism has six sides. To find the surface area of the prism, you add the areas of six sides. Can you see that opposite sides will have the same area? They have the same area because their length and width are the same. The formula for the surface area of a rectangular prism is SA = 2lw + 2lh + 2wh. The surface area of the prism above is

SA = (2 × 4 × 5) + (2 × 4 × 2) + (2 × 5 × 2)
= 40 + 16 + 20 = 76 inches

Finding Volume or Capacity

To find the volume or capacity of a rectangular prism, you use a **cubic unit.** A cubic unit is a unit of volume whose length, width, and height are the same. A **cubic inch,** for example, is 1 inch long, 1 inch wide, and 1 inch high.

The formula for the volume of a rectangular prism is

V = l × w × h

The volume of the prism shown above is

V = l × w × h = 4 × 5 × 2 = 40 cubic inches

This means that 40 one-inch cubes will fit inside the prism.

Pre-Algebra

Integers

Look at the two number lines below. The first one shows whole numbers. The second number line shows **integers**, a set of numbers that includes the set of whole numbers. The numbers to the right of 0 on the line are called **positive integers**. The numbers to the left of 0 are called **negative integers**. Whole numbers make up the set of positive integers and zero.

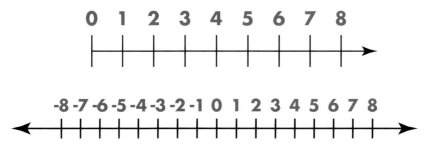

> When we write negative integers, we use a negative sign: -7. When we write positive integers, we can write a positive sign: +4. Usually, however, positive integers are written without a positive sign.

Every integer has an opposite. The opposite of 1 is -1. The opposite of -8 is 8. The opposite of an integer is also called its **additive inverse** because the sum of the two numbers is 0.

$$1 + {}^{-}1 = 0 \qquad {}^{-}20 + 20 = 0$$

Comparing and Ordering Integers

Look at the integers on the number line below. Notice that the opposites 1 and ⁻1 are the same distance from 0. The opposites 10 and ⁻10 are also the same distance from 0. The distance between any integer and 0 is the **absolute value** of the integer.

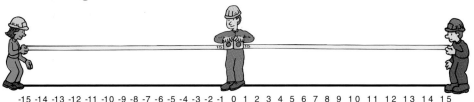

-15 -14 -13 -12 -11 -10 -9 -8 -7 -6 -5 -4 -3 -2 -1 0 1 2 3 4 5 6 7 8 9 10 11 12 13 14 15

The absolute value of 15 is 15.

The absolute value of ⁻15 is 15.

15 and ⁻15 have the same absolute value.

You can use the symbol || to represent the absolute value of a number.

$$|{^-}5| = 5 \qquad |58| = 58 \qquad |{^-}113| = 113$$

Integers on a number line increase in value as you move to the right. They decrease in value as you move to the left. When comparing two integers, ask yourself whether one integer lies to the right or left of the other on a number line. If it lies to the left, it is less than the other number. If it lies to the right, it is greater than the other number. This means that any positive integer is greater then any negative integer.

$$^-100 < {^-}1 \qquad {^-}5 < 0 \qquad {^-}1{,}000 < 1$$

Adding Integers

When you do calculations with integers, it is very important to note the signs of the numbers. If the integers you are adding all have the same sign, add the absolute values of the integers to find the sum. The sum will have the same sign as the addends. Adding the absolute values of positive integers is just like adding whole numbers. When adding negative integers, add them as you would whole numbers, but don't forget that the sum will also be negative.

$$8 + 4 = {}^{+}|8 + 4| = 12$$
$${}^{-}6 + {}^{-}5 = {}^{-}|6 + 5| = {}^{-}11$$

When you add integers with unlike signs, first compare their absolute values. Subtract the lesser absolute value from the greater absolute value to find the sum. The sum will have the sign of the number with the greater absolute value.

Adding a negative number to a positive number is like subtracting: The negative sign tells you to add in a *negative* direction. Instead of counting *up* on a number line, we count *down*. If we add 5 to 8 in a negative direction (moving to the left), we find a sum of 3.

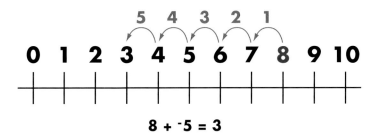

$$8 + {}^{-}5 = 3$$

Changing the order of the addends does not change the value of the sum.

$${}^{-}5 + 8 = 3$$

Subtracting Integers

To subtract integers with the same sign, compare the absolute values of the minuend (number being subtracted from) and subtrahend (number being subtracted). Subtract the integer with the lesser absolute value from the one with the greater absolute value.

If the absolute value of the subtrahend is less than the absolute value of the minuend, the difference will have the same sign as the minuend.

$$5 - 3 = {}^{+}|5 - 3| = 2 \qquad {}^{-}6 - ({}^{-}2) = {}^{-}|6 - 2| = {}^{-}4$$

If the absolute value of the subtrahend is greater than the absolute value of the minuend, the difference will have the opposite of the sign of the minuend.

$$3 - 6 = {}^-|6 - 3| = {}^-3$$
$${}^-4 - ({}^-7) = {}^+|7 - 4| = 3$$

To subtract a positive integer from a negative integer, add the absolute values of the minuend and subtrahend. The difference will be negative.

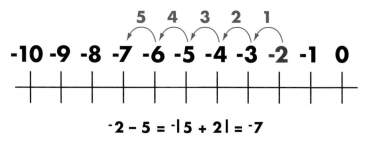

$${}^-2 - 5 = {}^-|5 + 2| = {}^-7$$

To subtract a negative integer from a positive integer, add the absolute values of the minuend and subtrahend. The difference will be positive.

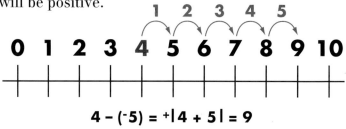

$$4 - ({}^-5) = {}^+|4 + 5| = 9$$

Algebra Is . . .

Algebra is a branch of mathematics that uses unknown numbers to solve equations. An **equation** is a number sentence that says that the values on both sides of an equals sign are the same.

$$6 + 4 = 10 \qquad 5 - 5 = 0 \qquad 9 = 3 \times 3$$

When mathematicians write equations in algebra, they use **variables** to represent numbers that are unknown. Letters are often used as variables.

$$5 - a = 3 \qquad 4y = 12 \qquad a + 4 = 12$$

Finding the value of a variable in an equation is called **solving for the variable**. Look at the equation below. From your addition facts, you know that $2 + 3 = 5$, so $x = 2$.

$$x + 3 = 5$$

You can also solve the problem using algebra. To solve the equation, you need get x by itself on one side of the equals sign. You can do this using the **inverse** of addition, which is subtraction. Subtracting 3 from the left side of the equation will get x by itself. Remember that an equation is a statement that says that two values are equal. If we change the value of one side of the equation, we must change the value of the other side by the same amount. Subtract 3 from the right side of the equation.

$$x + 3 - 3 = 5 - 3$$

Complete the calculations to find the value of x.

$$x = 2$$

Use the inverse of subtraction to solve the equation below for b.

$$b - 6 = 3$$
$$b - 6 + 6 = 3 + 6$$
$$b = 9$$

To check your work in solving an equation for a variable, substitute the answer in the original equation:

$x + 3 = 5$ **Substitute 2 for x.**
$2 + 3 = 5$
$5 = 5$

Since the two sides of the equation are equal, you know that 2 is the correct answer.

Solving Algebra Problems

Variables can also be used to solve equations involving multiplication.

Erica's company makes watercolor paint sets. In each set, there are 36 pots of paint arranged in four rows. How many pots are in each row?

You know the total number of pots of paint in each set (36) and the number of rows of pots (4). Use this information to write an equation with a variable. Let y = the number of pots in a row. Four times the number of pots in a row will give a total of 36 pots.

$$4y = 36$$

To solve for y, you need to get y by itself using an inverse operation. The inverse of multiplication is division, so divide each side of the equation by 4.

$$\frac{4y}{4} = \frac{36}{4}$$

(Remember that $\frac{4y}{4}$ is the same as $4y \div 4$.)

$$y = 9$$

There are 9 pots of paint in each row of the set.

Two-Step Equations

Solving algebra problems can take many steps. You have learned methods that will allow you to solve problems that take two steps.

The key to solving algebra problems that take more than one step is to do the calculations in the right order. The rule to follow in these kinds of problems is to simplify first by adding or subtracting terms, then by multiplying or dividing.

The problem below is a two-step problem. First, add 6 to both sides of the equation. Then, multiply both sides by 3.

$$\frac{b}{3} - 6 = 2$$

$$\frac{b}{3} - 6 + 6 = 2 + 6$$

$$\frac{b}{3} = 8$$

$$3 \times \frac{b}{3} = 3 \times 8$$

$$b = 24$$

Check your answer by substituting 24 for *b* in the original problem.

$$\frac{24}{3} - 6 = 2$$

$$8 - 6 = 2$$

$$2 = 2$$

For the problem below, subtract 3 from both sides of the equation. Then, divide both sides by 2.

$$2x + 3 = 21$$

$$2x + 3 - 3 = 21 - 3$$

$$\frac{2x}{2} = \frac{18}{2}$$

$$x = 9$$

Check your answer by substituting.

$$(2 \times 9) + 3 = 21$$

$$18 + 3 = 21$$

$$21 = 21$$

Algebra Word Problems

On Saturdays, Carrie and her sister look for new flowers to add to their wildflower collection. One day, Carrie found three times as many new flowers as her sister, but she lost six of the flowers on the way home. Carrie had 30 flowers when she got home. How many did her sister find?

The problem is asking you to find how many flowers Carrie's sister had, so let a = the number of flowers found by Carrie's sister. The problem says that Carrie found 3 times as many flowers as her sister, so we can write that number as $3a$ flowers. Carrie also lost 6 flowers, so the number she had when she got home was $3a$ - 6. The problem says this number was 30, so you can write an equation and solve for the variable.

$$3a - 6 = 30$$
$$3a - 6 + 6 = 30 + 6$$
$$3a = 36$$
$$\frac{3a}{3} = \frac{36}{3}$$
$$a = 12$$

Carrie's sister found 12 new flowers.

Check your answer by substituting it in the original equation.

$$(3 \times 12) - 6 = 30$$
$$36 - 6 = 30$$
$$30 = 30$$

Probability
and Statistics

Probability

Probability is the chance that something will happen.
Probability has many uses. You can calculate the probability
of a ticket being drawn in a raffle. You can calculate the probability of rolling a certain number on a pair of dice. Weather
forecasters use many sources of information to calculate the
probability of certain weather events, such as rain and snow.

In order to calculate probabilities, you need to know the **sample space.** The sample space for an experiment or problem is
all the possible results, or **outcomes.** For example, if you are
calculating the probability of drawing a ticket with a certain
number from a box containing 500 tickets, the sample space
is the 500 possible outcomes of the drawing.

An **event** is one part, or outcome, of the sample space. In the
example above, the event we are interested in is the drawing
of a certain ticket from the box. This event is called a **favorable outcome.**

Calculating Probability

The probability of an event is the ratio of the number of
favorable outcomes to the number of outcomes that are possible in the sample space.

$$P(E) = \frac{\text{number of favorable outcomes}}{\text{number of possible outcomes}}$$

P (E) means "the probability of event E."

The probability of drawing one particular ticket from the box can be expressed as the ratio 1/500. 1 represents the number of favorable outcomes. 500 represents the number of possible outcomes of the drawing.

You can calculate the probabilities of rolling certain numbers on a die (number cube). There are six numerals on a die (1, 2, 3, 4, 5, and 6), so the number of possible outcomes is six.

What is the probability of rolling a 3?

The number of favorable outcomes is one (rolling a 3). P(3) = 1/6.

What is the probability of rolling an odd number?

The number of favorable outcomes is three (rolling a 1,3, or 5). P(odd number) = 3/6 or 1/2.

What is the probability of rolling a 10?

The number of favorable outcomes is 0. P(10) = 0/6 or 0.

What is the probability of rolling a number less than 7?

The number of favorable outcomes is six (1, 2, 3, 4, 5, or 6). P(number < 7) = 6/6 or 1.

Statistics

Statistics are numbers that are used to describe a **population.** A population is an entire group of individuals. A population can be the people who live in a certain area, people who have certain characteristics or behaviors, a certain breed of cat, and so on. Statistics are based on **data,** or pieces of information, from a population. They represent facts about a group.

Finding Averages

One of the most commonly used statistics is the **average**. There are three different kinds of averages. The **mean** is the sum of all the data in a set divided by the number of items in the set. Another kind of average is called the **median.** To find the median of a data set, you need to rank the data in order of value—from least to greatest or from greatest to least. The median is the middle value if the number of items in the set is odd; it is the mean of the two middle values if the number of items in the set is even. The **mode** is the number that occurs most often in a set of data. Some data sets have more than one mode.

To find the mean, add the scores of all of the students. Then divide the sum by the number of students. To find the median, find the mean of the two middle scores. To find the mode, find the score that appears most often on the list.

Math Test Scores	
Bill	95
Nancy	95
Keisha	92
Alex	88
Ingrid	82
Jack	81

Graphs

Graphs are a helpful way to present data. It is sometimes easier to see patterns in data presented in a graph than it is to see them in long lists of numbers. Different kinds of graphs can be used to organize different kinds of data.

A **bar graph** makes it easy to compare different sets of data. This bar graph shows the populations of the five largest cities in the United States.

City	Population
New York	7,322,563
Los Angeles	3,485,557
Chicago	2,783,726
Houston	1,629,902
Philadelphia	1,585,577

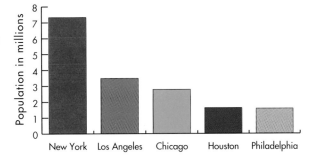

A **line graph** can be used to show changes over time. The line graph below shows how the population of a city has changed over the years, for example.

Year	Population
1950	7,891,957
1960	7,781,984
1970	7,895,563
1980	7,071,639
1990	7,322,563

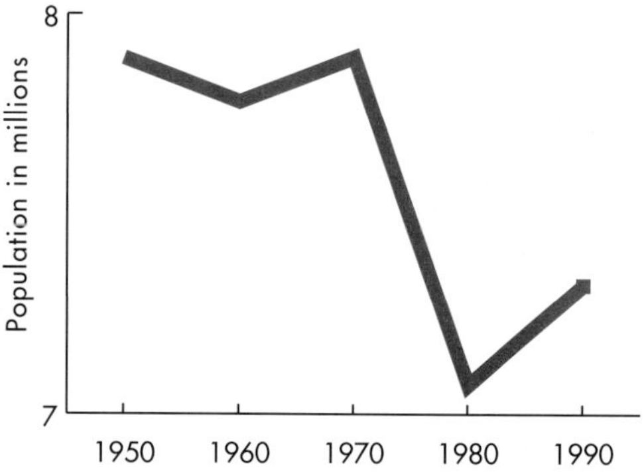

A **circle graph,** or **pie graph,** works best when you are comparing parts of a whole. The circle graph below shows the percentage of Americans who belong to different age groups.

Age	% of Population
0–9	15.2
10–19	13.7
20–29	14.7
30–44	24.7
45–64	19.6
65 and up	12.1

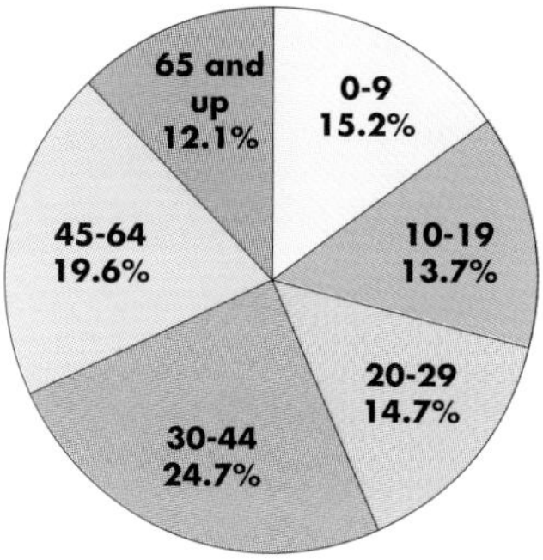

Index